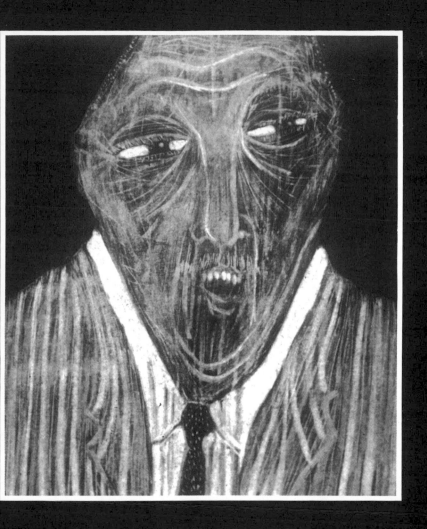

Essential Words

Copyright © 1985 by Seymour Mayne

Publication of this book was made possible by a grant from the Multiculturalism Directorate of the Secretary of State, though the views expressed do not necessarily reflect the position or policy of the Government of Canada. The editor and publisher also wish to acknowledge the generous support of the Samuel and Saidye Bronfman Family Foundation as well as that of the Jewish Community Foundation of Greater Montreal. The editor wishes to thank Sylvia Brown for helping him to verify texts and sources. Laurence Eldredge and David Staines were both generous with constructive comments. Finally, he is grateful to his wife Sharon for her patience and support in bringing this work to completion.

ISBN 0 88750 576 7 (hardcover)
ISBN 0 88750 577 5 (softcover)

Cover art by Seymour Segal
Typesetting and design by Michael Macklem

Printed in Canada

PUBLISHED IN CANADA BY OBERON PRESS

PS
283
J48
87
985

49,790

This book is dedicated to the memory of my aunts, Jennie Katz and Annie Saperstein.

5

6

INTRODUCTION

How does one recognize a Jewish poem or a Jewish Canadian poem? Not only by the subject or the individual voice of the poet, but also by a particular stance, an edge to the voice and an ability to apprehend and render the complexity of experience. Though both "Jewish" and "Canadian" seem to defy strict definition, Jewish Canadian poets on the whole are recognizable by their emphasis on the human dimension, the translation of the experience of the immigrant and the outsider, the finding of joy in the face of adversity, the linking with tradition and the concern with history in its widest sense. They strive for the essential words that echo more than the individual's need. They move to enter a communal language, to find the words that speak to and for the community, whether they relate to the everyday or the eternal. Their words draw in their contemporaries, while invoking the presence of ancestors and tradition.

Essential Words brings together the work of 34 poets whose achievement has been crucial, for more than 50 years, to the development of Canadian poetry. Jewish Canadian poets appeared on the literary scene at a critical time when the Canadian literary community began to sustain its own tradition. They turned to the communal fears and identifications of Canadian life, then to its positive features, its husbanding of energies and resources, its balance and equilibrium. The dominant direction of their writings has been shaped by an urban and psychological realism that focuses on the human, and on the poem as a well crafted yet urgent communication that must be shared if it is to be vital and memorable. In the ferment of conflicting literary groups—some drawn to what is fashionable abroad, others to the realistic depiction of the Canadian landscape and environment—Jewish Canadian poets have found their own way. The poetry they have written belongs to the literature of Canada while, at the same time, delineating a unique space of its own. They embody the best of the Canadian tradition, carrying it forward while remaining connected to their own sources.

Jewish Canadian poets did not have to assimilate their sensibility and poetics to an Anglo-Saxon or Anglo-American mainstream or identity. The same metropolitan pressures did not bear down upon them. A balance of identities, an eclecticism of poetics and an equilibrium of the private and the public voice marked their poetry, and the cultural mosaic of Canada afforded them a sure and intense sense of roots and independence.

Jewish immigration to Canada began in earnest after the assassination of Czar Alexander II in 1881 and the wave of pogroms that followed in its wake. The largest Jewish community in the country took root in Montreal. Sandwiched between larger English and French communities, it sustained its own social and educational institutions and remained almost autonomous in its religious and cultural life. This position gave the Jewish community a unique perspective. Neither English nor French, the writers who emerged from this milieu were particularly sensitive to the creative tension that nourished their best work because they were exposed to the multifaceted aspects of life in Quebec's largest city. In the early decades of this century the literary vitality of the immigrant community first found expression in Yiddish, and by 1934 H.M. Caiserman-Vital could write about the work of more than 40 poets in his pioneer study, *Jewish Poets in Canada*. Almost a dozen of the poets he discussed were writing in English, and these included three contributors—Hyman Edelstein, A.M. Klein and Shulamis Yelin—to this anthology.

In English Canada the poetic activity ushered in by the poets of the Confederation group began to lose its freshness and force by the time of the First World War. The modernist assault of the McGill poets—A.J.M. Smith, F.R. Scott and Leo

Kennedy—did not fully rule out the nationalist revival that followed the end of the war. This second phase of a growing native literature had to come to terms with an internationally inspired modernism and a growing Canadian self-awareness. At this juncture A.M. Klein, Canada's first major Jewish poet, appeared on the scene and joined the Montreal group.

At first, Klein interpreted his Judaic heritage and Jewish experience; then, from the mid-forties, with his awareness of history, his sense of roots and his passionate voice, he began to explore by analogy the world of French Canada. English Canada now had a poet who bridged the two official linguistic communities. It was no accident that it was a Jewish poet who fulfilled this task with insight and sympathetic understanding. At a time when Canadians needed to see themselves in their landscape and environment, Klein was the poet who helped shape Canadian self-awareness. His book of sustained social portraiture, *The Rocking Chair and Other Poems*, remains one of the few seminal collections of Canadian poetry. In poetic strategy and intent Klein prepared the ground for the growth of documentary and socially centred poetry in the decades that followed. He owed much to the ferment in Montreal in the forties. By learning from his peers in the *Preview* and *First Statement* groups, he was able to assimilate their techniques and approaches and surpass them. He celebrated his tradition, explored the Canadian milieu and probed the darker aspects of twentieth-century history. The rampant anti-semitism of the thirties, the destruction of European Jewry in the Holocaust, the founding of the State of Israel—these subjects he did not exclude from his imaginative work.

But Klein's world was touched with the tragedy of his reclusive years. The foreboding shadow of failure was hinted at or alluded to in both his poetry and his prose. As the first major Jewish writer of Canada, he was caught between the demands of his art and the needs of his community. No Jewish writer after him would have to face the dilemma in quite the same way. Although he may have despaired of the poet's function and work, he would certainly have rejoiced in the renaissance of Jewish writing in the seventies and eighties. As a Canadian and a Jewish poet, he grows in stature, and what he may not have pursued to completion in his own *oeuvre* may come to fruition in a generation of poets who were too young to have known him personally.

It was inevitable that the celebration of tradition and community would be challenged by a writer who would immediately follow Klein in the Jewish community of Montreal. If Klein represents one pole in Canadian and Jewish Canadian writing, Irving Layton launched its complementary opposite. For Layton, the Jew has always been the outsider. When Layton described the Jew as a "non-conformist by his very station in life," he was speaking as well of himself and his own role as a challenger of prevailing taste and decorum in Canadian literature. Not a man of the community as Klein was, Layton did not embrace a religious observance. The radical circles of Montreal in the thirties were his academies. From the early forties, when he began to publish and joined with John Sutherland and Louis Dudek in the *First Statement* group, he entered into polemics and debate that challenged the literary sensibility of English Canada. The inevitable clash of taste helped to liberate Canadian poetry. Critics found his urgency of voice and satirical thrusts strident and distasteful. Critical in his social awareness, Layton disaffiliated himself from accepted traditions and from the community. But he wrote from his roots and his experiences, which were shaped by a Jewish skepticism and urban openness. In fact, his aggressive and provocative approach was first hailed by Klein himself in a review of Layton's first book, *Here and Now*. Klein noted Layton's Jewishness, which, he said, "manifests itself more in his approach to a subject than in the subject itself," and that approach has stood in direct opposition to the mythopoeic, documentary and post-modernist poetics in Canadian writing. Layton has defined it as a skeptical and cosmopolitan attitude, a tough-minded earthiness, and its influence has spread well beyond the Jewish poets who were to follow him. He also found inspiration in the Jewish prophetic tradition, and from the sixties historical and moral themes come to the forefront in his work.

In the forties and fifties Klein and Layton shaped the direction of Canadian poetry with their best work. One cannot account for the development of Canadian poetry without examining the influence of these opposite yet complementary figures. Between them they laid the foundation for a tribe of Jewish poets who made Montreal their centre. The group includes Avi Boxer, Leonard Cohen, George Ellenbogen, Seymour Mayne, Malcolm Miller, Henry Moscovitch, David Solway and others. Although the primary figures were Klein and Layton, the contributions of other poets have added scope to the tradition their writings continue and develop.

Outside of Montreal Jewish Canadian poets, exploring the experience of the immigrant and the outsider, have also written affirming their roots and the possibility of communal identification in a country that was beginning to acknowledge the positive features of its multicultural life. Born in Winnipeg, Miriam Waddington has lived in Montreal and Toronto. In the forties she participated in the literary ferment in Montreal. Her early work reflects her lyrical response to life as well as her social concerns. Her later writings reach out beyond the self and articulate an involved response to experience and identity. She has attempted a variety of forms that younger poets have consciously or unconsciously sought to imitate, and her work has grown in strength and resonance. Like Klein, she has turned her attention to the contribution of Yiddish writers, both in Canada and elsewhere, and she has rendered their poems into fine and moving translations. She opened a dialogue with the vibrant and elegiac poetry of the poets of

Eastern Europe and enriched the language in her own poems as few of her American and English counterparts have done.

Following Klein, Layton and Waddington, the next generation of Jewish Canadian poets began to publish in the fifties. From the outset, Leonard Cohen and Eli Mandel expressed an ambivalence toward their roots, and after the initial explorations they turned away from the Jewish presence in their work. When they did return to Jewish subjects in later books, it was not with the richness and sense of detail evident in Klein's writings or the affirmation in the later poetry of Layton and Waddington. Perhaps Cohen and Mandel reflected the changes in the Jewish community of Canada as it made itself secure and assimilation began to take its toll.

Cohen's sensibility inhibited him from finding his place in a larger communal pattern. In a conscious attempt to widen the scope of his writing in *Flowers for Hitler*, he tried to universalize the alienation and victimization of the Jewish condition. As he broadened the range of his work, the particularity of identity was blurred and ceased to be either real or credible. In Mandel's poetry a similar development became apparent. His finest work seems to be wrested from the confusions and paradoxes of self-discovery. Struggling against the compression of the language and forms of his poetry written during the sixties, he revealed the pathos of the struggle and the ominous hold of his Jewish upbringing. His more open and experimental later poetry does not record the same degree of involvement, and the Jewish presence begins to fall away.

Although some poets stand apart from literary trends and from their contemporaries, they reveal other Jewish attitudes and approaches. Joe Rosenblatt's play with language and surreal fantasy draws some of its inspiration from Klein and Layton, and David Solway's work has an independence of spirit reminiscent of Cohen. Other poets remain on the periphery and show few overt signs of either their background or their heritage. In the poetry of Tom Wayman and Susan Glickman what has been distilled is a sensitivity and critical awareness that bring their work within the circumference of this anthology.

While Cohen's personal poetry was thinning itself out as reductive expressions of artistic self-doubt and failure, a new generation of poets emerged, drawing one step closer to Jewish subjects and themes. Avi Boxer and Phyllis Gotlieb, whose work first began to attract notice in the fifties and sixties, are followed by Seymour Mayne, Sharon Nelson and Joseph Sherman. Their writings draw them alongside Jewish poets working in other English-speaking countries.

These poets, who begin to publish in the sixties and seventies, are not concerned with style or poetic experimentation for its own sake. Nor do they simply emphasize statement or message. The balance of the private and public elements —almost a continuous touchstone of Canadian poetry—informs the work of these younger poets. They have not abandoned a full response to experience, nor do they limit their expression to one particular literary aesthetic; they cultivate what will draw out a balanced and complex utterance. They turn to Jewish and Judaic sources with greater self-confidence than their immediate predecessors, joining the many Jewish poets now writing in English who have stamped the language with the sensibility of a cosmopolitan community at ease in the English-speaking world and still at one with its own millenial tradition.

SEYMOUR MAYNE

STREET REVISITED

Avi Boxer

May fangs of lightning
strike me dead
if I ever forget
this slumlit street,
this red brick shack
that twisted my mother
into a cursing hieroglyph,
these windows that shuttered
my father's Mosaic light.

These are the xylophone fences
I strummed with a branch,
the sewers that hid me
from Jew-baiting gangs,
the rooftops that became my ship . . .

and here,
here in this secret lane,
still strewn with garbage
and disembowelled rats,
I first wept and learned to trade
childhood almonds
                    for bitter herbs.

NO ADDRESS

Avi Boxer

I am late.
I have missed the wedding.
My father descends
the synagogue stairs
with my dead mother
veiled in white.

What shall I do?
I cannot cross the street.
The traffic-lights will not change.
The snow falls like confetti.
They do not see me.
I shout.
They do not hear me.
Gone.

A talith of snow
slips from a branch
over my shoulders.
My hands tremble,
open before me,
like a prayerbook.

A patrol-car stops.
A policeman questions me,
discovers
I have no address.

YOM KIPPUR

Avi Boxer

O pray
for the holy fool
locked in the pillory
for his young wife
and bewildered sons
circling white roosters
above their heads.

O pray
for the false messiah
riding his donkey
through the city gates,
for the sackcloth poet
who turning to wood
in a philistine field
raised his tired arms
and burst
into the forgiveness
of straw.

O pray
for the stunned adulteress
I carried naked upon my shoulders
through the judicious marketplace,
for the jubilate congregation
that stoned her, judaized her
against the synagogue wall

and pray, pray
for my helpless name
rising from her torn throat
like a cactus

ABRAHAM AND ISAAC

Mick Burrs

I am posed beside my smiling mother
at the overhanging ledge,
among the knife-edged mountains.

At first no-one notices
my eyes squinting, wanting to close
here, in the Garden of the Gods.

You can see my small body
made smaller
by the polished lens
for the camera's sacrifice.

I am my father's subject
beneath the sun's lethal glare.

I grip my mother's arm.
That's my father's hand
brushing something away,
blotting my mother
out of the movie.

Annoyed by my fear,
he directs me
to open my eyes, wave
my arms, perform
some small memorable action.

My hands are clenched
at my sides, my eyes
closed down, the mountains
behind me falling for miles.

Look closely now as the mountains
begin to tilt and the clouds
vanish from the sky and I stand
sideways, filling up the frame.

Whirring, the camera
cuts in. Close. Closer.
My face bloats in the foreground.
My forced smile contorts.

See my eyes snap
open: how perfectly
they communicate

love, confusion, terror.

21

LISTENING

Mick Burrs

He sits there, listening.
He won't speak up. Doesn't have to. Just sits
in the armchair in the next room, his face hidden

behind a newspaper. Now I am saying
false things to my friends. My hands sweat, my face
burns, I want to end this talking, to tell them,

My father's here, listening.
I see through the doorway
his black shoes

shining before the armchair.
My friends get up to leave.
They walk past him.

I am left alone, listening
to my father's silence:

soon he will be telling me
(as he always does)
everything that's wrong.

I am a child
who cannot sleep in darkness,

my heart tapping
between four secret walls—

my eyes listening,
listening.

PRAYER FOR SUNSET

Leonard Cohen

The sun is tangled
   in black branches,
raving like Absalom
   between sky and water,
struggling through the dark terebinth
to commit its daily suicide.

Now, slowly, the sea consumes it,
leaving a glistening wound
   on the water,
   a red scar on the horizon;
In darkness
   I set out for home,
terrified by the clash of wind on grass,
and the victory cry of weeds and water.

Is there no Joab for tomorrow night,
   with three darts
   and a great heap of stones?

23

LAST DANCE AT THE FOUR PENNY

Leonard Cohen

Layton, when we dance our freilach
under the ghostly handkerchief,
the miracle rabbis of Prague and Vilna
resume their sawdust thrones,
and angels and men, asleep so long
in the cold palaces of disbelief,
gather in sausage-hung kitchens
to quarrel deliciously and debate
the sounds of the Ineffable Name.

Layton, my friend Lazarovitch,
no Jew was ever lost
while we two dance joyously
in this French province,
cold and oceans west of the temple,
the snow canyoned on the twigs
like forbidden Sabbath manna;
I say no Jew was ever lost
while we weave and billow the handkerchief
into a burning cloud,
measuring all of heaven
with our stitching thumbs.

Reb Israel Lazarovitch,
you no-good Romanian, you're right!
Who cares whether or not
the Messiah is a Litvak?
As for the cynical,
such as we were yesterday,
let them step with us or rot
in their logical shrouds.
We've raised a bright white flag,
and here's our battered fathers' cup of wine,
and now is music
until morning and the morning prayers
lay us down again,
we who dance so beautifully
though we know that freilachs end.

25

OUT OF THE LAND OF HEAVEN

Leonard Cohen

Out of the land of heaven
Down comes the warm Sabbath sun
Into the spice-box of earth.
The Queen will make every Jew her lover.
    In a white silk coat
Our rabbi dances up the street,
Wearing our lawns like a green prayer-shawl,
Brandishing houses like silver flags.
    Behind him dance his pupils,
Dancing not so high
And chanting the rabbi's prayer,
But not so sweet.
    And who waits for him
On a throne at the end of the street
But the Sabbath Queen.

Down go his hands
Into the spice-box of earth,
And there he finds the fragrant sun
For a wedding-ring,
And draws her wedding-finger through.
　　Now back down the street they go,
Dancing higher than the silver flags.
His pupils somewhere have found wives too,
And all are chanting the rabbi's song
And leaping high in the perfumed air.
　　Who calls him Rabbi?
Cart-horse and dogs call him Rabbi,
And he tells them:
The Queen makes every Jew her lover.
And gathering on their green lawns
The people call him Rabbi,
And fill their mouths with good bread
And his happy song.

For Marc Chagall

THE GENIUS

Leonard Cohen

For you
I will be a ghetto jew
and dance
and put white stockings
on my twisted limbs
and poison wells
across the town

For you
I will be an apostate jew
and tell the Spanish priest
of the blood vow
in the Talmud
and where the bones
of the child are hid

For you
I will be a banker jew
and bring to ruin
a proud old hunting king
and end his line

For you
I will be a Broadway jew
and cry in theatres
for my mother
and sell bargain goods
beneath the counter

For you
I will be a doctor jew
and search
in all the garbage-cans
for foreskins
to sew back again

For you
I will be a Dachau jew
and lie down in lime
with twisted limbs
and bloated pain
no mind can understand

29

TO A TEACHER

Leonard Cohen

Hurt once and for all into silence.
A long pain ending without a song to prove it.

Who could stand beside you so close to Eden,
when you glinted in every eye the held-high razor,
shivering every ram and son?

And now the silent looney-bin,
where the shadows live in the rafters
like day-weary bats,
until the turning mind, a radar signal,
lures them to exaggerate mountain-size
on the white stone wall
your tiny limp.

How can I leave you in such a house?
Are there no more saints and wizards
to praise their ways with pupils,
no more evil to stun with the slap
of a wet red tongue?

Did you confuse the Messiah in a mirror
and rest because he had finally come?

Let me cry Help beside you, Teacher.
I have entered under this dark roof
as fearlessly as an honoured son
enters his father's house.

ALL THERE IS TO KNOW
ABOUT ADOLF EICHMANN

Leonard Cohen

Eyes .... Medium
Hair .... Medium
Weight .... Medium
Height .... Medium
Distinguishing features .... None
Number of fingers .... Ten
Number of toes .... Ten
Intelligence .... Medium

What did you expect?

Talons?

Oversize incisors?

Green saliva?

Madness?

MASADA

Stanley Cooperman

1. Terms of Agreement

The function of a Jew
is to die.
That is his function;
or to survive wrapped in psalms,
violins,
rags
   money . . .
an object for your (discreet)
sympathy,
astonishment that still
he breathes, and walks,
refusing to settle
on the garbage dump of History
which
      kindly
you define, being ready
to forgive his existence.

The function of a Jew
is to splatter chicken-fat
on the smooth tables
the kitchens
the ovens
of your love:
the hunchback you entertain
who squats
              comic
on piles of his own dead,
wailing
under the moth-eaten canopy
of his beard: you give him more
than he deserves.

The function of a Jew
is to dance
like a soft-shoe beggar
with a bible stuck in his mouth,
greasy coins
between his fingers:
not for him the earth, not
for him
unborrowed sky . . .
the function of a Jew is
to be
        allowed.

33

2. Exile

"If I forget thee, O Jerusalem ... "
my father
dragged his shrivelled foot
all over Europe, remembering
white wolf rolling country
and the holy teeth
of Easter:
the child
with a crucifix
driven into his skull,
arms and legs
hung among the onions,
a tavern
      a street
an iron window
washed with the official ceremony
of blood.

34

It was embarrassing:
every week my father would take me
through a holy valley
of melted candles,
and toss me
                screaming
into his eyes . . .
it was a foreign country:
the names he remembered
fell out of his mouth like
dry stones,
and I carried my flesh
like a wall
against that flood
of the replaceable
dead.

35

"If I forget thee, O Jerusalem ... "
with all the silence
of my shaved and television face
I tried:
Shakespeare reminded me,
and Chaucer;
Dickens whipped me back
through streets of bleeding sewers,
Eliot convinced me,
Pound
scraped me off the peeling walls
of his old man's prison:
I held each book
with a handful
of circumcised fingers.

36

3. The Wedding

We were married in Teheran
under brown mountains
that curled around the ears
of a Unitarian minister;
his horn-rims
flashed in the sun,
carpets were rainbows for our feet . . .
afterward we celebrated
with a small party:
a sociologist, a poet, an information officer
from the Embassy
who toasted us in champagne,
two black marines
who brought girl-friends,
unpinned their medals
and drank rum:
(we were street-brothers, having shared
a night when women
swirled around our pockets
and laughter poured from our glands) . . .
at the party the marines were still laughing
though I did not
yet
know why:
I danced past their secret skin
like an acrobat

37

That week we arranged
a road of paper
to take us through the world:
Greece and Italy, Paris, England . . .
where we belonged, where
we came from; visas stamped, miles approved,
our eyes
were Technicolour, brochures
filled our suitcases: and then
THE HOLY LAND
CITY OF GREAT RELIGIONS
a magic paste
of camels, crucifixions and
tombs.

38

4. The Tourist

After tea at the YMCA,
after smiles
Idaho
conversation, when even the bacon
was blond,
we walked toward Jerusalem:
I held my camera
like a bullet-proof vest,
our guide
twirled his dry moustache
and glittered at his pilgrims.

It was 24 hours
after I had signed a paper
that I had no "Jewish blood" . . .
the man at the Embassy
said
he had no control,
the eagle behind his desk
had no control,
and I dipped my pen in gall
being good, being agreeable, being
what was necessary
to be
a pilgrim
to the holy city of Jerusalem.

When we arrived at a wall
where goats
fed on their own excrement,
our guide paused, wiped his sleeve
and smiled:
"a Jew place" he said
pointing to the inscriptions,
tatters of cloth,
30 centuries of tears
eaten into rock;
"they came to cry" he said
wrinkling, and we
the pilgrims
smiled back, nodding,
hanging out of our teeth,
comforted, familiar:
the lady from Idaho complained
of the smell.

Later
we climbed the Mount of Olives
pious; the road was holy,
sweat beaded our skin like rosaries,
and all around us
stones lay on the yellow earth,
burial urns
with their names painted out,
red paint smeared over their verses:
from Minsk and Alexandria,
Cracow, Berlin:
old men had come to be buried . . . .

I watched them
scream under the earth,
their beards
opened like empty hands, their eyes
filled with mud,
with thorns:
our guide watched me
and I
watched my face.

41

5. Homecoming

The function of a Jew
is to die.
That is his function;
that
    was
his function: we have come home,
and if we die
it will be without your permission,
and without your love:
we have tasted your love
and it burned us . . .
it flows through the world
like a sewer of used blood.

Listen: our hands are no longer empty,
and our dreams
are of olive groves,
oranges
planted on the edge of despair;
if we die
it will be here,
if we die
it will be as the lion dies
protecting his young.

YAHRZEIT: FOR THE WARSAW GHETTO FIGHTERS

Stanley Cooperman

Let each hand turn into a tree:
let the screams become flowers,
a rainbow
planted in the earth . . .
yesterday is poison fruit:
let tomorrow
be blue as morning.

Who remembers their names,
the small men
beaten into iron,
twisting prayer-books
into fists?
Zachariad Artstein, his shadow
nailed against the sky
like a flag . . . .

Do you think they died?
Walk among the orange groves
blossoming
on the edge of the sea:
the young men with music
in their bodies,
their women
stronger than despair.

43

What was done
in that April of madness
lives in our flesh:
let our arms
shape
a harvest of bright grain:
remembering,
we shall be nourished.

THE CROSS ON THE HILL

Hyman Edelstein

Beside his newsstand on the curb
Where the wild crowds tear past,
Or wait, and flee for the tram-cars homeward,
An old Jew shivers against a pole
That towers above him with its top be-crossed . . . .

The snow is hard and cold under his feet,
His small son, between blowings of his ungloved hands,
Serves the papers, and clutches the pennies,
And over all
High from the Hill shines white the glittering Cross.

The groaning tram-cars speed their burdens home . . .
And now but straggling passers pick a paper or two . . . .
The bitter wind sweeps down from the hill,
And blows a frozen Jew against a pole
As if impaled . . . .

HEP! HEP! HEP!

Hyman Edelstein

("When to the ears listening for the signals of the Messiah,
the Hep! Hep! Hep! of the Crusaders came like the bay of
blood-hounds: and in the presence of those devilish mission-
aries with the sword and firebrand the crouching figure of the
reviled Jew turned round, erect, heroic, flashing with sublime
constancy in the face of torture and death"—George Eliot.)

Hep! Hep! Hep!
And Israel heard:
The fiends swept madly on—
He never stirred.

Hep! Hep Hep!
Pealed in his ear:
The fiends were at his back—
He did not fear.

Hep! Hep! Hep!
The outcast, spurned,
Despised of men, to meet
Death, torture turned.

Hep! Hep! Hep!
Like as a rock,
He stood, defied, repulsed
The seas' wild shock.

. . .

Perished their arm and sword,
But not their stain
Who took the name of the Lord
And a Jew in vain.

JUST ANOTHER WHISPER

George Ellenbogen

In this time of not-yet famine
when children are going mad
with blood and bone
            and murder on the parlour rug
when adults are playing chess
with guns drums and the young
and death fails to discriminate
between colours or flags
the harvests of the young
turn grey
and the old
         lacking youth
are not worth two whispers
in the winds
         of their economic battlefields
The rains destroy all records
so that even the recorders
are unable to make distinctions
And as the machines move
in a routine of ignorance
one feels somehow that
in this season
         when oil replaces blood
         and bones become
steel spikes
death will not wait for a show of hands

NAMING THE DRAGONS

Susan Glickman

Always the same silence.
After nimble, defiant discussion of everything
else—two women in a room at night
inside the porcelain cup
of winter, two women working overtime
to understand their lives—
the word *men* hits the floor like a smoke-bomb,
a grey perplexity in which we lose
our way.

If only the baby would cry now
to give us some focus.
If only we could arrive at some stop-gap summation
to let us quit the confessional
with grace.

There's never an easy way out
to know our dark brothers:
what they keep from themselves they also keep
from us. Night after night
we anatomize ourselves
looking for Adam's rib, the thing they fear they've lost
by giving themselves to us.

How we confront that fear in them each time,
each time we hope to fearlessly
go on. How we stand over the torrent
watching the house wash away—
how there's never any bridge,
how we must learn to build one over and over again.

The things we thought were simple, bed and board,
shift their shapes in moonlight
to dragons of venom and steel.
Money and work, the monsters of everyday,
crawl tamely past like sensible household pets.

For Mary di Michele

48

ISHMAEL

Artie Gold

Ishmael (you clever little fellow)
you really know how to frighten a guy
you fix on me with one eye
with the other
stare inward till your scalp
soaks your brain's scarlet up.

have your youth
have your little joke
but get older quickly
    and join us
   I'm frightened just thinking
at anything naive as you
If you suddenly saw
   the president of the United
   States coming at you with a hatchet
you'd yet find it in your child's heart
               to forgive him.

49

PHRASE-BOOK

there is too much wrong with this soup for me to accept it

the women of the city break my heart

I know I will always be a foreigner

ON THE ROAD

Phyllis Gotlieb

I see you, Ben Ezra, looking up
through rents in bent
umbrellas, laughing at
lightning *if I*
sold shrouds no-one would die heel spark
dance on gravestone every
cemetery a park *and ai!*
if I sold lamps
scroll weary of scruffy
starmap and snappy
tips for the strolling
tzadik *if I sold lamps you'd see*
the sun stand still
from spite!
stay up all night!

a stunning, rueful miracle

50

MEMENTO

Phyllis Gotlieb

They said: you are not afraid of
death; go in there get your father's
tallith. It is in the
bottom drawer, in the lefthand
corner, in the velvet bag
with the mogandavid.

The lamp was still on, he
still slumped on the bed
greyfaced in the sick light.

The tallith is a prayer-shawl, a piece
of silk with stars and fringes
made in factories, by human hands
like any coat or shirt.

Do tallithim wear out? I know
when I hold one, that it will cover
a dead man's shoulders.

51

A COMMENTARY

Phyllis Gotlieb

Good morning, the old man says
good morning toward the
yeshiva in heavystep
bookbag clasping
books in black letters blacker
than the ovens of Auschwitz lettershapes
crimped round thought/tongues of fire
his eyes are
wetstones
his beard splayed, in shoe heavystep
he smokes, breathes, breathsmoke
pillars the air
good morning:
melamed,

on Saturday morning
melamed, good Shabbas, he
brings home a minyan
of Hasidim for l'chaim

l'chaim!

in black:
caftans, fur shtreimlach: white
stockings: swung sidecurls:
pink flesh: black
asphalt green leaves: yellow sunlight blue
sky they come
step: walk
in a black flock pass

52

from pane to pane black
brown pink white black brown pink
white betweengreen
aisles of glass

when I go by the school where
minds may be narrowed I see
the yard a hundred Jewish children
laugh yell and raise hell
red blue green yellow

eyes like washed stones
splayed beard, a bringer of Hasidim
spreads the leaves of his prayers for them
: *this is an aleph*
his children have succumbed to Cyclon B

the old man smiles
good morning

good morning!
                    from Lubavichi, Lublin
Bratzlav, Berditchev: Berlin
from Modzitz, Mezrich, Bialystock
Fastov, Opatov, Lodmir, Lodz

: ghostmarch in the noon of night
from pane to pane black brown pink white
betweengreen
aisles of glass

53

LATE GOTHIC

Phyllis Gotlieb

From the window of my grandfather's
front room above the store I could see
over the asylum wall through the barred window
a madwoman raving, waving
pink arm sleeves. From the kitchen at the back
faceted skylights lay, grown quartz among the sooty
stalagmite chimneys. Two faces of despair.

My grandmother and grandfather cultivated
in the scoured yard of their love
a garden of forget-me.

My grandmother was a golden
turbulence, my goldwin, giver of all
lovehated vortex. Like all children I looked
twenty-five years later at her picture and found
the woman, monstrously coarse and obese
a drowned reaching beauty.

My grandfather, crumpled old Jew, read Hebrew
through a magnifying glass, crawled
to the park for sun, swore, told old tales
babbled of green fields and died.

My father sold that legendary
furniture for twelve dollars
                          and we smelled the stench
of the furs the old man had made his shapeless coats of
and went down the narrow walled stair for the last time
into the bright street between the wall upflung
against the howling chimney of the madwoman's throat
on the one side
and the redbrick rampart of shoddy stores against the
reaching blackened arms of the chimneys on the other.

55

CENACLE

Phyllis Gotlieb

ah Lord, what's that bunch up to now?
Simon says it's the last time he'll have them in the house
Simon says abc one day and xyz the next
only thirteen he says, thirteen
not counting the women, them
pecking their noses in my pots, rolling matzot
in my kitchen, soldiers
slamming shields on the door
yelling for food I hadn't got, servant girl
running out to the well and caught there
coming with torn skirts and swollen eyes
mouth twisted she won't tell, oh
I can tell you, soldiers
feed these thirteen, says Simon
where was I to get money for meat, Lord, meat?
not looking at me Simon says
pock nose stubbed leper hands
feed them
Lord, I sold my carcase to the butcher for their meat
thick bloody fingers ripping the flanks in two
into my flesh
ripe tastes better, he tells me, nails sharp as his knives

I know where blood flows
thirteen
hangdog the lot of them on the way to a bad end
in my upper room, never raised eyes to me
serve them
this their festival? one says
I will be betrayed   what wonder? flesh
Lord, sacrificed for the meat
that one I felt bad for, had it in his face
and the other worse, with the eyes: *I will betray*
the one: *my body, my blood the bread and wine*
and the rest cried for him
                        I don't begrudge weeping
and I know trapping
but that sick-eyed one, alone, my Lord, I know
the body and blood

57

MORNING AFTER THE FIFTY MEGATON

K.V. Hertz

If, in some plain
the moon had scratched against the sky
spewing red ash
I cannot tell.
When I awoke I saw no wound
but only the subtle places
   on the kitchen's floor
where the fine red sand
   falling all night from
   the monster-breeding air
had gathered,
   unseen to everyone else.

And inside my morning's egg
   before I cracked it
   with the sharp and metal spoon
I nightmared torn dragons
pulsing and breeding;
torn from the shape
   they might have borne—
the cracked the scalp-curved shell.

The sun was there; there
   and playing on my fingers
   in an oblong
   white upon enamelled cupboard doors
as if doom were nothing
but some German pedant's
                     metaphysical gout
   and was not falling
             falling
   through my broiling skin.

59

PARABLE

K.V. Hertz

When he was young
it seemed as if a century
had hunched his back
into a buzzard's
low-slung stance.

Hunched on his bed
he grew a parable:
a strange deep-eyed bird
he sent to wrestle
with the heated clouds.

Thrown there
by gusts of burning wind
thrust downward
by the wings' ascending rage,
its cries beat madly
against his ears;

until his bird,
scorched into a blackened wreath
whirled murderously toward him,
the hollow sun
grasped tightly
in its broken beak.

LANDMARKS

George Jonas

After sixteen years I remember you
Ossington bus, O'Leary Avenue.

Perhaps gravity makes them loom so large
West Lodge, St. George Street, York garage.

Northcliffe backyard, where cops used to appear
after midnight to confiscate my beer

or Glenholm boarding-house, five bucks a room,
whose dome languidly crumpled into doom

and bursting water-pipes had drowned in steam
the ex-mate of a German submarine.

The beanery on Queen Street where a lame
girl first sat in my booth and asked my name.

Or long before, a metal winter night,
a funeral home's sign casting a light

flickering blue on grey December slush:
with cardboard trunks, torn clothes, needing a wash,

an evil-smelling strange boy, tall and thin,
had asked to spend the night. And god knows why

they took me in.

ONCE MORE

George Jonas

Kirov was shot, Solon will rot in jail,
even the smallest hold-up man will hang,
Eichmann has died seven times, but the real,
the real murderers all live in my street.

They go to work each day at eight o'clock.
Some take the bus, some drive, and many walk.
They have a child or two, they like a smoke,
their wives wear rings, Sunday they cut the grass.

They talk about the business, the weather,
there is a faint click as they lock the door.
Only a few of them would hurt a fly
and all of them support a family.

Will they be caught? Is theirs the perfect crime?
All I see is the circle of the time,
all I know is I have to be prepared.

Caution causes me to glide through the walls
at night and stand beside them just to see
how long they have to wash their hands before
they turn the light out and they go to sleep.

HOTEL ROYAL, 1970

George Jonas

The April wind is gentle.
The socialist sky is blue.
Our limousine is waiting.

My friend the film director pans toward me
and stops with his innocent eyes in extreme close-up.
He informs me he's happy.

He is happy in a happy country,
free, creative, and soon he will drive
to his island retreat in his East German car.
He dollies back for a final goodbye
and fades out slowly.

The April wind is gentle
the socialist sky is blue
the limousine waits patiently.

A shabby woman steps into the frame,
informs me she has not eaten for three days
and asks me for five *forints.*

I wave at my friend and smile,
and give the woman three *forints,*
and get into my limousine.

They are probably both lying
and I've become too old to chase after
the whore of truth in strange cities.

COMPASSION

Gertrude Katz

When my father woke, his morning prayer
    trembling on his lips
thanking God almighty for his manly birth,
    I cursed.

When my mother woke, her childbirth sheets
    ripped with pain
and cursed the almighty God for her maternal stain,
    I scoffed.

Now I: woman, wife, mother,
    neither scoff nor curse
but speak gently of childbirth
    to men.

A STYLE FOR DYING

Gertrude Katz

I thought the world ends
with a whisper, Pa

reluctant, the soul flies away
from bones left shaking

in sacks of flesh
gently goodnighting away—

is that only for Welsh country
gentlemen? no rage

in their heritage gifts?
Oh, your deathbed style

needs recording, Pa—how you
powered your hulk, shook your head

raised a fist once more
in Hebrew anger

dismissing tears—my fears
fled through the door

you thundered: "I will decide
when I'm finished!

Hold up the gallon cup
I drank dry—

who doesn't like stains
I left there

can piss on my grave
when I die."

Then I heard you shouting
for the Angel

demanding he come get your soul.
Seventy-seven years undefeated

even He couldn't cross
your stubborn will.

66

PSALM XXII: A PRAYER OF ABRAHAM, AGAINST MADNESS

A.M. Klein

Lord, for the days allotted me,
Preserve me whole, preserve me hale!
Spare me the scourge of surgery.
Let not my blood nor members fail.

But if Thy will is otherwise,
And I am chosen such an one
For maiming and for maladies—
So be it; and Thy will be done.

Palsy the keepers of the house;
And of the strongmen take Thy toll.
Break down the twigs; break down the boughs.
But touch not, Lord, the golden bowl!

O, I have seen these touched ones—
Their fallow looks, their barren eyes—
For whom have perished all the suns
And vanished all fertilities;

Who, docile, sit within their cells
Like weeds, within a stagnant pool.
I have seen also their fierce hells,
Their flight from echo, their fight with ghoul.

Behold him scrabbling on the door!
His spittle falls upon his beard,
As, cowering, he whines before
The voices and the visions, feared.

Not these can serve Thee. Lord, if such
The stumbling that awaits my path—
Grant me Thy grace, Thy mortal touch,
The full death-quiver of Thy wrath!

PSALM XXVII: A PSALM TO TEACH HUMILITY

A.M. Klein

O sign and wonder of the barnyard, more
beautiful than the pheasant, more melodious
than nightingale! O creature marvellous!

Prophet of sunrise, and foreteller of times!
Vizier of the constellations! Sage,
red-bearded, scarlet-turbaned, in whose brain
the stars lie scattered like well scattered grain!

Calligraphist upon the barnyard page!
Five-noted balladist! Crower of rhymes!

O morning-glory mouth, O throat of dew,
announcing the out-faring of the blue,
the greying and the going of the night,
the coming on,
the imminent coming of the dawn,
the coming of the kinsman, the brightly plumaged sun!

O creature marvellous—and O blessed Creator,
Who givest to the rooster wit
to know the movements of the turning day,
to understand, to herald it,
better than I, who neither sing nor crow
and of the sun's goings and comings nothing know.

PSALM XXXVI: A PSALM TOUCHING GENEALOGY

A.M. Klein

Not sole was I born, but entire genesis:
For to the fathers that begat me, this
Body is residence. Corpuscular,
They dwell in my veins, they eavesdrop at my ear,
They circle, as with Torahs, round my skull,
In exit and in entrance all day pull
The latches of my heart, descend, and rise—
And there look generations through my eyes.

69

THE CRIPPLES

A.M. Klein

Bundled their bones, upon the ninety nine stairs—
St. Joseph's ladder—the knobs of penance come;
the folded cripples counting up their prayers.

How rich, how plumped with blessing is that dome!
The gourd of Brother André! His sweet days
rounded! Fulfilled! Honeyed to honeycomb!

Whither the heads, upon the ninety nine trays,
the palsied, who double their aspen selves, the lame,
the unsymmetrical, the dead-limbed, raise

their look, their hope and the *idée fixe* of their maim—
knowing the surgery's in the heart. Are not
the ransomed crutches worshippers? And the fame

of the brother sanatorial to this plot?—
God mindful of the sparrows on the stairs?
Yes, to their faith this mountain of stairs, is not!

They know, they know, that suddenly their cares
and orthopedics will fall from them, and they
stand whole again.
                    Roll empty away, wheelchairs,
and crutches, without armpits, hop away!

And I who in my own faith once had faith like this,
but have not now, am crippled more than they.

(Oratoire de St.-Joseph)

70

GRAIN ELEVATOR

A.M. Klein

Up from the low-roofed dockyard warehouses
it rises blind and babylonian
like something out of legend. Something seen
in a children's coloured book. Leviathan
swamped on our shore? The cliffs of some other river?
The blind ark lost and petrified? A cave
built to look innocent, by pirates? Or
some eastern tomb a travelled patron here makes local?

But even when known, it's more than what it is:
for here, as in a Josephdream, bow down
the sheaves, the grains, the scruples of the sun
garnered for darkness; and Saskatchewan
is rolled like a rug of a thick and golden thread.
O prison of prairies, ship in whose galleys roll
sunshines like so many shaven heads,
waiting the bushel-burst out of the beached bastille!

Sometimes, it makes me think Arabian,
the grain picked up, like tic-tacs out of time:
first one; an other; singly; one by one—
to save life. Sometimes, some other races claim
the twinship of my thought—as the river stirs
restless in a white Caucasian sleep,
or, as in the steerage of the elevators,
the grains, Mongolian and crowded, dream.

A box: cement, hugeness, and rightangles—
merely the sight of it leaning in my eyes
mixes up continents and makes a montage
of inconsequent time and uncontiguous space.
It's because it's bread. It's because
bread is its theme, an absolute. Because
always this great box flowers over us
with all the coloured faces of mankind . . . .

MEDITATION UPON SURVIVAL

A.M. Klein

At times, sensing that the golgotha'd dead
run plasma through my veins, and that I must live
their unexpired six million circuits, giving
to each of their nightmares my body for a bed—
inspirited, dispirited—
those times that I feel their death-wish bubbling the
channels of my blood—
I grow bitter at my false felicity—
the spared one—and would almost add my wish
for the centigrade furnace and the cyanide flood.

However, one continues to live, though mortally.
O, like some frightened, tattered, hysterical man
run to a place of safety—the whole way run—
whose lips, now frenzy-foamed, now delirium-dry
cry out the tenses of the verb to die,
cry love, cry loss, being asked: *And yet unspilled
your own blood?* weeps, and makes
his stuttering innocence a kind of guilt—
O, like that man am I, bereaved and suspect,
convicted with the news my mourning breaks.

Us they have made the monster, made that thing
that lives though cut in three: the severed head
which breathes, looks on, hears, thinks, weeps, and is bled
continuously with a drop-by-drop longing
for its members' re-membering!
And, the torn torso, spilling heart and lights
and the cathartic dregs!
These, for the pit! Upon the roads, the flights
—O how are you reduced, my people, cut down to a limb!—
upon the roads the flights of the bodiless legs.

Myself to recognize: a curio;
the atavism of some old coin's face;
one who, though watched and isolate, does go—
the last point of a diminished race—
the way of the fletched buffalo.
Gerundive of extinct. An original.
What else, therefore, to do
but leave these bones that are not ash to fill—
O not my father's vault—but the glass case
some proud museum catalogues *Last Jew.*

73

RHINE BOAT TRIP

Irving Layton

The castles on the Rhine
are all haunted
by the ghosts of Jewish mothers
looking for their ghostly children

And the clusters of grapes
in the sloping vineyards
are myriads of blinded eyes
staring at the blind sun

The tireless Lorelei
can never comb from their hair
the crimson beards
of murdered rabbis

However sweetly they sing
one hears only
the low wailing of cattle-cars
moving invisibly across the land

74

THE FINAL SOLUTION

Irving Layton

It's been all cleared away, not a trace:
laughter keeps the ghosts in the cold ovens
and who can hear the whimpering of small children
or of beaten men and women, the hovering echoes,
when the nickelodeons play all day the latest Berliner
love ballads, not too loudly, just right?
Taste the blood in the perfect Rhenish wine
or smell the odour of fear when such lovely
well scented frauleins are fiddling with the knobs
and smiling at the open-faced soldier in the corner?

History was having one of its fits—so what?
What does one do with a mad dog? One shoots it
finally and returns armless and bemedalled
to wife and children or goes to a Chaplin film
where in the accommodating dark the girlfriend
unzips your fly to warm her hands on your scrotum.
Heroes and villains, goodies and baddies, what
will you have to drink with your goulash? In art museums
together they're shown the mad beast wagging its tail
at a double-hooked nose that dissolves into ash

And appraised by gentlemen with clean fingernails
who admire a wellexecuted composition or pointed to
in hushed tones so that nothing of the novel frisson
be lost. Europe blew out its brains
for that frisson: gone forever are the poets and actors
the audacious comics that made Vienna and Warsaw
hold their sides with laughter. Gone, gone forever.
They will never return, these wild extravagant souls:
mediocrity stopped up their witty mouths,
envy salted the ground with their own sweet blood

Sealed up their light in the lightless halls of death.
Alas, the world cannot endure too much poetry:
a single cracked syllable—with a cognac—suffices.
I have seen the children of *reingemacht* Europe, their
queer incurious dead eyes and handsome blank faces,
leather straps and long matted hair their sole madness.
They have no need of wit or extravagance, they have
their knapsacks, their colourful all-purpose knapsacks.
The nickelodeon grinds on like fate, six fatties play cards:
the day is too ordinary for ghosts or griefs

76

OSIP MANDELSHTAM (1891-1940)

Irving Layton

I once did an hour-long TV show reading
from your *Stamen* and *Tristia*: out there
were my compatriots who had never before
heard of your name and pain, your nightmare fate;
of course the impressario spoke impressively
about your stay in Paris where you mastered
the French symbolists, your skill as translator
(what pre-Belsen Jew hadn't promiscuously
shacked up with five or six gentile cultures)
the Hellenic feeling in your prose and poems
—to be brief, he filled in the familiar picture
of enlightened Jew ass bared to the winds

But when that self-taught master symbolist
il miglior fabbro put you on his list of touchables
that was the end; you perished in the land waste
of Siberia, precisely where no-one knows and few care
for in that stinking imperium whose literature
you adorned like a surrealist Star of David
you're still an unclaimed name, a Jewish ghost
who wanders occasionally into enclaves
of forlorn intellectuals listening
for the ironic scrape of your voice
in the subversive hum of underground presses

77

I know my fellow-Canadians, Osip;
they forgot your name and fate as swiftly
as they learned them, switching off
the contorted image of pain with their sets,
choosing a glass darkness to one which starting
in the mind covers the earth in permanent eclipse;
so they chew branflakes and crabmeat gossip make love
take out insurance against fires and death
while our poetesses explore their depressions
in delicate complaints regular as menstruation
or eviscerate a dead god for metaphors;
the men-poets displaying codpieces of wampum,
the safer legends of prairie Indian and Eskimo

Under a sour and birdless heaven
TV crosses stretch across a flat Calvary
and plaza storewindows give me
the blank expressionless stare of imbeciles:
this is Toronto, not St. Petersburg on the Neva;
though seas death and silent decades separate us
we yet speak to each other, brother to brother;
your forgotten martyrdom has taught me scorn
for hassidic world-savers without guns and tanks:
they are mankind's gold and ivory toilet-bowls
where brute or dictator relieves himself
when reading their grave messages to posterity
—let us be the rapturous eye of the hurricane
flashing the Jew's will, his mocking contempt for slaves

78

ISRAELIS

Irving Layton

It is themselves they trust and no-one else;
Their fighter planes that screech across the sky,
Real, visible as the glorious sun;
Riflesmoke, gunshine and rumble of tanks.

Man is a fanged wolf, without compassion
Or ruth: Assyrians, Medes, Greeks, Romans,
And devout pagans in Spain and Russia
—Allah's children, most merciful of all.

Where is the Almighty if murder thrives?
He's dead as mutton and they buried him
Decades ago, covered him with their own
Limp bodies in Belsen and Babi Yar.

Let the strong compose hymns and canticles,
Live with the Lord's radiance in their hard skulls
Or make known his great benevolences;
Stare at the heavens and feel glorified

Or humbled and awestruck buckle their knees:
They are done with him now and forever.
Without a whimper from him they returned,
A sign like an open hand in the sky.

The pillar of fire: Their flesh made it;
It burned briefly and died—you all know where.
Now in their own blood they temper the steel,
God being dead and their enemies not.

REQUIEM FOR A.M.KLEIN

Irving Layton

I remember your cigarette-stained fingers
The rimless glasses that glinted with your wit
And the bowtie protruding
Under your chin like a spotted tongue

Your scholar's mind neat as your hair
And the jaunty self-loving complacencies
That made me think of plump pumpkin seeds
Falling from your mouth, the epigrams

I finally gave up counting
Scattering like the pigeons on St. Mark's Square
When a piston ring suddenly explodes.
I still wonder at your psychological obtuseness

And the sentimentality each clever Jew
Misconstrues for sensitivity:
Fool's gold which you, O alchemist,
Changed into precious metal, solid and true

Warm-hearted egotist, my dear unforgettable Abe,
You were a medieval troubadour
Who somehow wandered into a lawyer's office
And could not find your way back again

Though the reverent adolescent
Like the Virgil which fee-less you taught him
Would have taken your hand and led you out
Muttering the learned hexameters like a charm

Now grey-haired I diet, quarrel with my son,
Watch a young girl make love to herself
Occasionally speak to God and for your sake
Resolve to listen without irony to young poets

But still muse on your bronzed tits of Justice.
Yes, here where every island has its immortal bard
I think of you with grateful tears and affection
And give them your fresh imperishable name

FOR MY BROTHER JESUS

Irving Layton

My father had terrible words for you
—whoreson, bastard, *meshumad*;
and my mother loosed Yiddish curses
on your name and the devil's spawn
on their way to church
that scraped the frosted horsebuns
from the wintry Montreal street
to fling clattering into our passageway

Did you ever hear an angered
Jewish woman curse? Never mind the words:
at the intonations alone, Jesus,
the rusted nails would drop out
from your pierced hands and feet
and scatter to the four ends of earth

Luckless man, at least
that much you were spared

In my family you
were a *mamzer*, a *yoshke pondrick*
and main reason for their affliction and pain.
Even now I see the contemptuous curl
on my gentle father's lips;
my mother's never-ending singsong curses
still ring in my ears more loud
than the bells I heard each Sunday morning,
their clappers darkening the outside air

Priests and nuns
were black blots on the snow
—forbidding birds, crows

Up there
up there beside the Good Old Man
we invented and the lyring angels
do you get the picture, my hapless brother:
deserted daily, hourly
by the Philistines you hoped to save
and the murdering heathens,
your own victimized kin hating and despising
you?
        O crucified poet
your agonized face haunts me
as it did when I was a boy;
I follow your strange figure
through all the crooked passageways
of history, the walls reverberating
with ironic whisperings and cries,
the unending sound of cannonfire
and rending groans, the clatter
of bloodsoaked swords falling
on armour and stone
to lose you finally among your excited brethren
haranguing and haloing them
with your words of love,
your voice gentle as my father's

MISTER SEBAG-WORTHER

Norman Levine

Mister Sebag-Worther
A well fed figure
The picture of Clemenceau
(So I am told)
Has given fifty years
To deciphering scratches
Made on stone.

Three universities
Four societies
Two governments
Have provided enough
Scholarships and Fellowships
To have kept him—
His wife—
And four children afloat.

He is now compiling a text to prove
That the scratches reveal a concern with food.

DAVID

Eli Mandel

all day the gopher-killing boys
    their sling-shot arms
       their gopher-cries

the king insisting
   my poetry must stop

I have written nothing since May

instead
      walk among the boys
gopher-blood on their stretched
hands
      murder will end murder
the saying goes, someone must
do something about the rodents
and poems do not:
          even the doctors
admit that it's plague
ask me about my arms
        look
at my shadow hanging
   like a slingshot

the world turns like a murderous stone
   my forehead aching with stars

85

PSALM 24

Eli Mandel

I no longer want to see
those terrible corrections
underlined with the red ink
of crab-apples bleeding on the lawn.

Take away your Talmudic trees
commenting on the stone Torah of our streets.

Isn't it enough that I've failed?
Do you have to indulge in this melodrama
of snowstorms and black poppies?

What did you expect?
You, who drove me to mad alphabets
and taught me all the wrong words.

It's your scripture. You read it.

CHARLES ISAAC MANDEL

These uplands of the suburban mind,
sunlit, where dwell the lithe ironists,
athletic as greeks, boy-lovers,
mathematical in love as in science.
Formalists. What have I to do with them?
I gather the few relics of my father:
his soiled Tallis, his Tefillin,
the strict black leather of his dark faith.

SNAKE CHARMERS: IN MEMORY A.M.K.

Eli Mandel

one, toothless, twirls his gown
around an aroused cobra's eye
another whips his own Medusa head
at an alarmed serpent
         here
Djemma el Fna, marketplace,
my childhood rises in that charmer's eye,
silks, spices, glittering coins, candied cakes,
all sway before me in this man's vertigo,
his mad mouth frothing at the snake's tongue,
his song, asides to casual drummers and to flutes,
his sideways step as quirky as the serpent's
lunge, strike like an old flint, an old lamp,
a wick
        Abraham Klein, Irving, Leonard,
you and I could once have sung our songs
here before these snakes, those Arab men
and for these same Jews from Paris or
New York
        Baghdad   Teheran   Jerusalem
Fez
   tales of the prophet and his magic horse

while wretched   blind   crippled
through eternal mellahs crawl
Jew upon Jew
                    the world's
great serpents
                    from that darkness
dazzled
          how

by chance   or graceful song

88

ON THE 25TH ANNIVERSARY OF THE LIBERATION OF AUSCHWITZ

Eli Mandel

the name is hard
a German sound made out of
the gut guttural throat
y scream yell ing open
voice mouth growl
              and sweat
"the only way out of Auschwitz
is through the chimneys"
                 of course
that's second hand   that's told
again   Sigmund Sherwood (Sobolewski)
twisting himself into that sentence
before us on the platform
                the poem
shaping itself late in the after
noon later than it would be:

Pendericki's "Wrath of God'
moaning electronic Polish theatric
the screen silent
            framed by the name
looking away from/pretending not there
no name no not name no

89

Auschwitz
in GOTHIC lettering
the hall
a parody a reminiscence a nasty memory
the Orpheum in Estevan before Buck Jones
the Capitol in Regina before Tom Mix
waiting for the guns
waiting for the cowboy killers
one two three
Legionnaires
Polish ex-prisoners Association
Legions
their medals their flags

so the procession, the poem gradual
ly insistent beginning to shape itself
with the others
walked with them
into the YMHA Bloor & Spadina
thinking apocalypse shame degradation
thinking bones and bodies melting
thickening thinning melting bones and bodies
thinking not mine/must speak clearly
the poet's words/Yevtyshenko at Baba-Yar

there this January snow
heavy wet the wind heavy wet
the street grey white slush melted concrete
bones and bodies melting slush
saw
with the others
the prisoner
in the YMHA hall Bloor & Spadina
arms wax stiff body stiff unnatural
coloured face blank eyes

                    walked
with the others toward the screen
toward the picture
                    SLIDES
        this is mother
        this is father
        this is
                the one who is
waving her arms like that
is the one who
                    like
I mean running with her breasts bound
ing
        running
                with her hands here and there
with her here and
                        there
hands
        that   that is
the poem becoming the body
becoming the faint hunger
ing body
            prowling
                    through
words the words words the words
opening   mouths ovens
the generals smiling saluting
in their mythic uniforms god-like
generals uniforms with the black leather
with the straps and the intricate leather
the phylacteries and the prayer-shawl
corsets and the boots and the leather straps

and the shining faces of the generals in their boots
and their stiff wax bodies their unnatural faces
and their blank eyes and their hands their stiff hands
and the generals in their straps and wax and stiff
staying standing
                    melting bodies and thickening
                    quick flesh on flesh handling
                    hands

        the poem flickers, fades
the four Yarzeit candles guttering one
        each four million lights dim
my words drift
                    smoke from chimneys and ovens
        a bad picture, the power failing
    pianist clattering on and over and through
the long Saturday afternoon in the Orpheum
        while the whitehatted star-spangled cowboys
            shot the dark men and shot the dark men
            and we threw popcorn balls and grabbed
            each other and cheered:
                                    me jewboy yelling
for the shot town and the falling men
            and the lights come on
                                and
        with the others
standing in silence

the gothic word hangs
over us on a shroud-white screen

and we drift away
>to ourselves
>>to the late Sunday Times
>>the wet snow
>>the city

>a body melting

Memorial Services, Toronto, 25 January, 1970
Y MH A Bloor &Spadina

93

ZALMAN

Seymour Mayne

The name was curiously given.
Both families agreed the firstborn's
would be chosen from the mother's side.
Her father's name? No, he may still be alive—
May '44—if the Nazis hadn't killed him yet.
Who knew of his end then?
                              But the mother's mother,
Zlateh—she who had married twice
and amassed money and means—
a boy named after a woman? Was it a forbidden thing?
And the name rooted from the Marranos
and hidden observance: Zalman;
Suleiman—did they know of the Turkish origins?
Not drawn from the Pentateuch,
no, a name of the orient, the eastern Diaspora
and linked in the beginning, the first consonant,
with a grandmother whose only lasting image:
the block of stone carved with Hebrew
in Bialystok's cemetery and her youngest son,
the uncle, standing there in the photo
just weeks before Poland fell—
the rest of her brood caught in a burning synagogue
before they could buy passage to New Jersey or Montreal.

She was dead then, her ears stopped
with that terrible silence marking its way
from the din of outrage—the flames licked the night
and the polish and german murderers
prepared for a Saturday night off, the air incensed
with smoke of scrolls and flesh.
Enough, we begin again, the father said, name him.
She will live.
                    —On their lips and in my face.

95

ZEYDEH

Seymour Mayne

Why didn't I think of it before—
to call you up on the other
side of the *Kaddish*
To speak pleasantries in Yiddish,
the only language you read
beside the candelabra burnished
by candleflame on *Shabbat* eve
You who had little sanctifying good
to say about your sons or wife

But you had one terribly deaf ear
To the other you held
a bone listening-horn curved
like Sherlock's smart meerschaum

Silent you always gave
the wisest answer—your snore,
muffled now
under an insulating stone
and somewhere in the centre of Montreal
in a snowy cemetery
your remaining smile
disintegrates with the bone

I who carry your forehead
by way of your youngest
wait for the Jerusalem sun
here to blot out
my face's dark rills
I am the other speaking face
of your eternally senescent smile

I hunt for clues,
remember who took
me by the hand thirty years ago
explaining how Yarushevsky's
wide corpse was to be washed
then clothed again and watched over
until the light rose
with the loud wail of the Laurentian
morning and its clamouring insects

97

BIRTHDAY

Seymour Mayne

Fallen in the Jewish Wars
a young man who will never age
shares the same prayerful eyes
of ancestors and our common birth
this day of May
—spring's point of no return
Son and brother still he lies
beneath shrubs and lettered stone
Though unknown to me his name
is on his father's lips,
his face before his mother
Today, our day, celebrating
my right hand has not forgotten
the cunning promise of script

For Shulamit Nardi

THE ARAVA: TO THE SINAI

Seymour Mayne

Everything is near
   at hand—
The sand and caked
   aridity
stretching from Yamit
   to Ophira

At the crossroads
   resurrected again
we put the essential words
on the tongues of men,
on the lips
   of those who despair
of speech and must ape
the cybernetic voice
which winds billions
and the future
past rock, bone
   and blood

99

2

May the surreal
   cities collapse
and become the diminutive
rubble of this desert

In its depth
   a stream
bursts forth
Somewhere in an unmapped
   spot
the water speaks out
   where springs
the unknown blood

100

3

I have come
from the templed centre
built up toward the height
where desert and plain
    meet
on the city's eastern ridge
and silently
wage the elemental
war of stone and water

Here the desert begins
to claim me
The papers in my pockets
fade as into sand
I pass into the enormous
tunnel of desert light

The words drop off
one by one
marked patrolmen
at the end of the line

I give my eyes
to the sun
here where the earth
flames into the near
    invisible

4

I am on the third
   side of the moon
populated only by the spars
spies of my people
They who crossed over
the fateful northern stream
   heading south
Who chose this direction
with Abraham
in the very nexus
   of the east

5

Way past the seventh well
   silence's resonance
      cracks the Negev's
      cratered moon

6

Here pattern is
the breath of the absolute
Spirit and wind
bereft of vegetation
become angels
Voice
begets silence

7

Diaspora
    upon diaspora—
We dispersed
    and came together

The voice speaks still
out of the caked earth
the desert's cliffs
the scales
    and stone tablets
The voice
    is the parched tongue
    and breath
    of silence

When you come down
from the distant summit
bring the stone
carved with living rites

103

EXECUTIONS

Malcolm Miller

the beauty of women
                    clatters upon me
    their slanted ankles at street-corners
        stampede me to bits
                        as they laugh
        through their ingenious hair the wind
            blows my heart like a buzzsaw
                            rampant
            amid my flesh and bone
        one half smile or one
                        casually aimed eye-boom
            I am run down in heavy traffic
                the beauty of women
            flickered through bus windows
        hands in black gloves
                        and pensive mouths
            grinds me like a coffee-bean
I would offer my life to unreal gods
to speculations
                in serene bibliotecs
    but the librarian has tropical breasts
        I crash from them
                        as from a cliff
    the beauty of women applying lipstick
        drowns me in blood
                        their compacts
        click shut and whish
                        my head
            drops into the basket

WHAT THE HASIDIM SAY

Malcolm Miller

We Hasidim say
when the messiah comes
he will blow a silver horn
and we will then rush into the streets
half-dressed and singing
to take our places
on the back of a gigantic whale
which will proceed in about two minutes
to Israel where henceforth
clothes and other necessities
    will grow on trees;

after the evening prayers I loiter on the curb
and follow the gowned
    and bearded rabbi home,
asking small troublesome questions
like how will our leather-soled shoes grip
the slippery sea-back of the whale,
and what if when He blows the horn
we are under a shower or in an airplane;

"it's all worked out,
    it's all worked out," he says
hurrying through the ghetto streets
"don't bother yourself";
but I, Leib Mendel Bekowsky, I do.

THE LIST

Henry Moscovitch

Someone is sitting
down next to me.
He is neatly dressed
and speaks
all the languages
of our city.
Will he spare me
when the revolution
comes
and my name
too
appears upon the list?

YOUR BREASTS

Your breasts
your lips
explain me
like a commentary.
Your warm
embrace
is the book
I read
while I court
the world.
Be with me
while I tell
our story
a thousand times.

CHANNALEH

Sharon H. Nelson

and we said always: channaleh
diminutive: small anna
and referred so to the cripple as if
her short leg must cut her stature by a cubit
or some biblical metaphor that attached to the mutilated
before christ came to drag them with the cross up that hill

oh channaleh, what did you know of religion, theology
grand-daughter of some great rabbi who also paced
up the hill, up the hill of sanctity
in a maroon silk robe to dance with angels, struggling
to force the Hand
of channaleh, you who came of a long line of dancing rabbis
were the first lame one in a family that hallowed
with the pounding of feet, the slap of hands

oh channaleh
what dreams did you have
of someday, cured and perfect walking
straight up the aisle to the canopy
or dancing in Moscow, Vilna, Montreal aux points

channaleh, channaleh, might you have been a gypsy
walking the length of the firmament
bringing joy with full breasts and skirts swinging
if you had not been wished upon us with this deformity
that caused sorrow in the heart of your mother
and was a thorn in your father's purse

channaleh, channaleh
what dreams did you have
in your bed in the night with no candle
the one short leg laid out straight and stiff as if
it didn't belong on your body

oh channaleh, like some
prosthetic appliance it lay
cool in your bed
it separated itself from you
it had
a life of its own
you
followed it
limping along or around or behind it
wishing it would atrophy, fall off, leave you in peace
to be whole
silently bearing with what resignation
even the diminution of your small name

thus distinguished
you limped also toward the furnace
as fast as the short leg would carry
they pushed you aside in haste for
the promised bowl of soup, clean bed, the holiday
no-one expected

you saw them go
your short leg
could take you no faster
you were
left behind
no whip, no prod
could sting through the pain of again being separate

the sergeants and corporals
seeing your longing
left you to die
not even worth burning

and when that leg
would take you no farther
you crawled after
with what longing to rejoin your derisive community
and no man would marry you

but on all fours you tried
to catch them up
who were by then
thin wisps of smoke

thus you traversed the country
doubly bent with pain and longing

of all your family of holy dancers
only you, channaleh, small cripple
survived

109

RITE OF PASSAGE

Sharon H. Nelson

I

long as a forced daffodil's green stem,
long as a lily's throat, and strong,
the necks of the daughters of Israel

long
as Penelope's skein

long
as Persephone's reign

long
as Rapunzel's mane

the hair of the daughters of Israel

remember the braids
mother taught you,
hand on loving hand
to plait

the knot, the curl, the twisted swirl;
each flow damned, each strand exactly placed

soft
in a way
that nothing else is soft

coarse
in a way
that nothing else is coarse

full
in a way
that nothing else is full
the flow, the shimmer and
the weight

each loose strand
an insurrection

III

3

you bow your head
force mine back
over the chair

my hair
undressed
hangs to the floor

it
breathes

a sound so delicate
we barely hear

(but mother,
how could you do this to me, mother?)

we smile
join hands,
pin the kerchief round

4

I/Eye/Ayee
a keening cry
across the centuries

each Jewish bride
scissored; her pride
guillotined, lopped off

long
as Lilith's exile,
Jezebel's curse

the hair
of the daughters of Israel

5

we sweat, pot-bound,
in the kitchen's heat,
our kerchiefs knotted,
tight, inelegant

in the room beyond
the celebration grows

grandfathers, uncles, neighbours
clap and pound

the fathers and the husbands
dance

6

i dream
a daughter

strong-
necked

long-
haired

YOU WHO ASK

Nathan Ralph

Your hands are
flare signals of anger
throttling
air—wishing it were me . . .

for injustice
sits puckishly on my lips
like a schoolboy
leader of a crime
who escapes untouched . . . .

Hatred burns your lips
until they're white
from reined-in, perilously
stampeding epithets you'd
like to hurl at me.

I.P.L.

Nathan Ralph

Your hair askew
And madness dancing in your eye—
A prim powdered jaw
Now angular with determination . . .

At last! My friend,
Brave enough to break
The bonds, that tie with crimson
Fluff . . . so comfortably.
Arid lands
Meekly nourished strong teeming buds
Created
To seed in the winds of the world
And blossom into
Throbbing truth and strength.

No sentimental song, no schoolboy dream
You sing—
Strength and animal spirit burst
As cruelly as nature
The thousand rules of etiquette
And small smugness
You eat rapaciously, live rapaciously
And sing rapaciously
My friend

116

FOR THE FIRST SARA, EREV YOM KIPPUR 5733

Janis Rapoport

Tomorrow
it is permitted
they will let me **mourn,**
light your candle
proclaim
the yiskadal and yiskadash
remember myself prismed in your **green eyes.**

Today
my belly swollen **with**
Sara reincarnate
I return to coffee grinds, horoscopes, the Tarot pack
as I tear
the last, whitened **hair**
from my scalp

117

PESACH 5735

Janis Rapoport

Earlier than April
the sun speckles
albino filaments of caviare
along the horizons of the windshield.
Jeremy wonders
why the moon's roundness spins as
proportionately westward as we travel east,
trailing translucent strands across
the twilight. Estayr sleeps
but Sara says,
with the Cartesian wisdom of a two-year-old:
because I am,
therefore you are.
When we arrive
at the long Seder table,
the crystal goblets already
brimming with Dali's rubies,
prism aural rainbows
while we wait, patient, in Egypt,
for Elijah.

ICHTYCIDE

Joe Rosenblatt

My uncle was Sabbath crazed
wouldn't flick a switch on Saturday
but on the caudal fin of Friday evening
he'd be cutting up Neptune's nudist colony
into mean kingdom cutlets.
On Friday, Uncle Nathan lowered a butterfly net
to catch an Alcatraz shadow
dreaming myriads of muscled minnows:
spice cuisines of Esther Williams—fish pornography.

Lips ellipsing; a spiny Baptist lay on newspaper
blue leviathan with chopped-up vertebrae
fanned fins in vendor's prayer
while scaly fingers mummified the prophet
—a fish head conjured Salome in a basket—

I too have knifed the sacred fish
have carnivored to please my palate:
a bass from a Chinese steam-bath
lay in a puddle of soya sauce.
This stranded swimmer on his oval casket
balanced death on optic centres;
animal penumbra expired for post mortem
I ghouled my way to the neck bone
then turned away from the Last Supper
for the eyes of Moby illuminated
or were they the fish eyes of Uncle Nathan?

Sleep, Uncle Nathan, sexton in Narwhale's synagogue!

UNCLE NATHAN SPEAKING FROM LANDLOCKED GREEN

Joe Rosenblatt

Wide, wide are the margins of sleep
deep, deep, deep in the flowerbox earth
I sleep . . . sleep . . . sleep . . . .
In Carp's ethereal tabernacle
micron lips crackle
spirit embryos gestate
grow jinx wings, umbilical fins, slit gills
cold heart, lung and lizard's spine
as from a cyanide backbone
flux of shadows strum . . . spiritons
from Death's encrusted harp.
Nephew, in this world
no dust remains, no nickel photos of our bones.
We are beyond dust
where spiritons and atoms hum
around a perfect planetary sun
—such is spectral sex—
from worm to fluorescent penetrant
in the grave, we all swing polar umbra.
Oye, so vengeful is Death's metamorphosis
that I go reincarnated in a minnow's whisper
who once dwelt as a barbaric fishmonger;
and now who can measure my sad physique?
                                        Givalt!
or catch my whisper on a spectograph.
Yet more soul-pinching than worm's acetylene:
There is no commerce in the Netherworld.

Earth Momma, forgive me
for every fish I disembowelled was a child;
there is no Kaddish for aborted caviare.

Earth! Earth! is the bitch still green
liced with people and Aardvark powers?
And my shop on Baldwin Street
does it stand? . . . damp and sacred as the Wailing Wall
under the caterpillar'd canopy of God?
Or has my neighbour swallowed up my Carp shrined
    enterprise
wherein I cradled images from Lake Genneserat
to fish fertiled ladies with halvah tongues
who shred my serpents into shrimp bread,
for fish food oscillates an old maid's chromosomes!
Carp, pickerel, transmogrified
where swimmers have been tranquilized
stomach's the body's palpitating madrigal.
God bless the primate's primeval stretch
but O to touch . . . touch . . .
a moon's vibration of a silver dollar
to see the fish scales rise and fall
before Lent's locust of Friday's carnivores.
Nephew, heaven is on Earth; above me
the sky is smiling like a White fish.
Its eyes are the moon and the sun.

THE SHELL GAME

Joe Rosenblatt

Passing by the Jewish Funeral Home
(for I always set the time by the clock
in the living-room)
I suddenly encounter the orbs of Mr. Z
the albino spectre
with a beard of laughing moonlight;
Z is emanating ectoplasm
a kind of chemical spirit heat.
Years ago Mr. Z had fitted my uncle into a walnut;
I helped carry the shell to a midnight limousine.
The casket was weightless
or was Z playing a shell game on Sunday?
Now glaring at me through a window
more sinister than Kafka's cockroach
are the walnut eyes of Z.
In the darkness of Mr. Z's palm
I lie quiet as a hopper
in a psychedelic matchbox
so peaceful
you can hear a fly sneeze
and then . . . a gust of warm air—
a voice squeezes through an eye-dropper:
"For twelve hundred bucks
which shell is the poet under,
MR. DEATH?"

THE BULLET-PROOF JEW

Joe Rosenblatt

I've been absorbing the luminations of Metamorpho
there's tears running through my fingers
so everything I touch turns lachrymose;
the hand of pathos grips me from a comic strip
where God in Metamorpho dwells in technicolour;
Dear reader: there's wondrous sublimation
beyond your scope of comprehension
as Metamorpho changes to a body of hydrogen
but I mere mortal can not float
with Metamorpho into the atmosphere,
escape the ennui on earth.
If I could rise like a spirit from a shawl
I'd trade my original Capt. Marvel comic book
to be that floating Jew in the ionosphere
                                        and bullet-proof.

For Al Purdy

123

NOT TO BE BORNE

Helene Rosenthal

It was easier
to recognize him as my father
after he had died.

Visitor in dreams
he came to offer his child,
firstborn daughter
the sudden world he'd found
he couldn't bear
to leave.

I remember on his deathbed
how he ran
barefoot through the tall fields
to his mother
crying to be healed;
how he returned
to the empty village in Galicia
and found her gone.

Nor was I comfort
earlier or
too late.   Hate nursed
the hurt inside
the factory of the new world
damned
his pulse. His veins
stitched pants together
threaded
the machine with protest.
Blue serge, khaki
trod him, herringbone
and twist and common drill
on Mr. Dunkelman's parade-ground;
where the drum-
majors were all union
executives
who raised production, piece-
work rate
that sapped his frame.

125

I didn't know the boy
dying, or the man
impersonating life who tried
to share it from the grave.
All I could do was promise
to try and live
without return, a different way—
but he'd back off
from my breathing bed
his gift of envy
scalding
both of us
with gall.

Family portrait. Everyone in separate
rooms. Him in the living-
room hunched over the radio. We seldom
saw his face; we lived
snowbound most of the year, other seasons
raging in us, while snow fell
steadily in him,
quieting
his summer impulse;
old country time
              come to a city stop;

. . . each dawn the conscript drudge
rewound into the rhythm of
the shop: Tip Top Tailors
where he trudged a
quarter-century, *Gehenna* he
brought home each night. Cold supper
even *Yahveh* wouldn't eat
with us on Friday, shabby
shabbas of our
lost Israel.

So it wasn't real,
his going, as his coming . . . .
No tears fell,
the final grave
too deep
for human sympathy
and he was indifferent
to flowers.
Birds he loved.
But what good am I to him
now?
To tell the truth,
what lingers
more real than epitaph, is
that the only growth
he ever experienced
was cancer.

127

THE GUIDE

Nancy-Gay Rotstein

He drives his car
wherever They tell him
to Masada or Bethlehem,
Ben Yehuda or Hayarkam.
He jokes in five languages
English, Arabic and Italian,
German when necessary.
He plays his cassette,
Goodman or Shaw
for his Americans
and Caruso for others.
He opens doors,
waits in marble lobbies,
explains history tirelessly.
In his pocket, a Gun
on his arm, a Number
in his heart, Steel.

VALLEY OF JEZREEL

Nancy-Gay Rotstein

Armageddon,
you have called
out your warnings
to all nations
yet you lie laden
with fruits and cotton,
resting your blood-stained soil.
Saul, I hear your anguish
echo from mountain peaks
and sweet Deborah
your trumpet's call.
Through the mist
shadows of French,
British and Turks march
to the clash of drums.
But now rest,
sleeping Jezreel, rest.

129

WEDDING POEM

Ray Shankman

At my wedding
there was no red-haired
madman fiddling,
no Uncle dancing with two bottles
of shnaps cradled in his arms,
no Grandmother hiking up her skirts
to dance the Blackbottom;

At my wedding
there were 100 plates invited:
how many from our side
how many from that side
arguments over which is better
square tables or round tables,
friends I've never seen
mooching a meal underneath the Circus tent;

A silly photographer who grieved
when the Bride wouldn't smile
a supercilious Rabbi who droned text
without feeling, a mother whose iron will
never melted before the potential
of Divine Union.

At our wedding
we had flowers and tears,
this egomaniac of a Bridegroom indignant
full of passionate conviction screaming
to the guests, "I hope you'll all be as happy
as we are going to be" and a pissed Aunty
shouting back, "we'll wait and see, we'll wait and see."

At our wedding
the song ended before it began;
the dance faltered before the mirror
of wilting flowers and tearstained makeup
and the guests, now dead, plotted the marriage course
with deft fingering minds.

THE TEST

Ray Shankman

I read how you Abraham
saddled your own ass
and bound your own son
simply it is told
you were taking your son
your only son who you loved up
to study TORAH
                 What is this movement
of sacrifice? Do we know the tears:
yours, Isaac's, Sara's?
How you have to go out and up
for the word and then that knife!
the hand raised
              the angel staying it
leaving my story suspended
shattered by an innocent ear
and a small voice,
              "Would *you* do that, Daddy?"

THE NAMING OF NAMES

Joseph Sherman

I am Jonathan
Or could have been
But for my great-grandfather
Who was dead

Named for the sound of a name
Instead of blood
I might have been
But for my grandmother
Who insisted

I am Jonathan
Or could have been
But for my mother
Who complied

Eight letters in my name
Instead of six
I could have had
But for my father
Who compromised

I am Jonathan
Or could have been
But for me
Who would not cleave in two

133

FATHERS AND SONS

Joseph Sherman

And Abram, whom God would rename Abraham in his 99th year, destroyed the idols made and worshipped by his father Terach

This son of Terach
has been listening
to another voice
again

    Note his eyes
    which are wild and bright
    not
    from revering the Chaldean night sky
    but from some veiled incandescence

Ah Avrom
beware
of wild bright-seeming promises

And were you incited
to inaugurate
some less-than-ancient rebellion?

Is this why you raise your stave to us?
Sweep us from your father's shelves?
Make a storm of our brittle bodies
upon your father's floor?

134

We have names Avrom
names mined from the oldest of canticles
older than the Euphrates

We attend to your prayers—
All the power put into our making
rises within us (Have you forgotten
how we were made?)

What does your new god call himself
and what does he promise you?

There is surety with us—
We will not send you out
to hostile lands
to forsake Terach's blood

He found us over Ur
in the stars
and in the moon

Clay shaped (to echo these
our patriarchs) we are but
the flesh of the old night

      But the spherical stones
      are gone from your eyes

      Your full hands mock us
      as your broad feet trample us

Almost
we can conceive the child
pain

And a thousand fragments
lie piecemeal
upon your father's floor

     Ah Avrom
     Avrahom
            a thousand gods

See
already
the children
scrabble for us
         begin
to pocket our voices

136

SARAI

Joseph Sherman

I was beautiful when we came into Egypt
where my husband called me sister
that he might live
and we might prosper

Yet
     though I toiled with him
I was without blemish
and my beauty was extolled
to Pharaoh Amenemhet

In his great city was I praised
My husband blessed by wealth

And in the evening
in a garden
comely women bathed me
anointed me
whispered Pharaoh's love-pledge
in my ear
        and sang
how I was lovely above all women

My husband
     when he came
kissed me as a brother
but gripped me as a bridegroom
wordless in his prayers

While in his eyes
                    there burned
the same light
as burned in Amenemhet's

And the women caressed me
with their plumage
and I was led to his chambers
where crouched his gods
        where
                as he made to approach me
the blood was blown from his face
and his eyes pierced by fiery thorns

His cries were a bitter anthem

And I was restored to my husband
who
        summoned by the priests
healed the Egyptian king

                            Each
knowing anger and shame
in the embers of the other's eyes

Stone touched stone
as we left that mighty city

138

Talons brushed my cheek

We went up from Egypt into the Negeb
into Gerar
whose king was Abimelech

And I was beautiful

139

OF TONGUES

Joseph Sherman

Of the berries
found in these woods
I like best
the one whose taste
I am unable to name—

my daughter
discovered the fruit
and assures me
of its exquisite
sweetness.

I have yet to master
the intricacy
of pronunciation
though I listen
intently—something
in the way one furrows
tongue with teeth—

meanwhile
she grows plump
and I spend my time
looking
within Hebrew texts
for the appropriate
blessing.

SURVIVOR

Kenneth Sherman

The animals
they marched in
they marched in
by two ees two ees . . . .

Forget the rhymes.
This is a matter of life
and death.
We are being saved.

"What for!?" stormed Noah, starboard,
fed up with lice and heaps
of shit-caked straw.

There was talk of mutiny.

His wife no longer slept with him.

He'd found one of his sons
diddling a baboon.

And night after night
his mindscape filled,
tumultuous, dark,
a chorus of shrieking heads
bobbing on the white froth.

Dreadful dreams
long after the sun shrank the seas
and a heavy silence settled on the world

long after the wide rainbow squatted
and long after the Lord of Fluids
made new promises.

First thing off the boat
Noah planted a vineyard

    and he drank of the wine
    and became drunk
    but it was no use.
    He was a ruined man,
    his 600-year-old head
    filled with rain

    with the wild eyes of children
    going under

GHOSTS

Kenneth Sherman

Poland is overrun
with the ghosts of three million Jews.

They are in the churches
hovering above thin white candles;
they are in the homes, in the steam
rising from barley soup.

Their faces look out from the
fireplaces lovers sit before

from the clear lakes and rivers
men fish in.

In the city of Warsaw
their disembodied voices
still bicker in the markets,
laugh in old theatres.

What is the life-expectancy
of a ghost?

In Spain, where the ghosts
are 500 years old,
their faces are less definable
their screams fainter

and by the ruins of the Second Temple
they are simply light
upon stone.

COROLLARY

Steve Smith

And so it is like in
Pharaoh's dream
only here the fat
swallow the lean

And through their
big bellies
the lean
pass away
into flesh . . . .

O ye fat men
you have eaten
my lean and God-
hungry people.

144

GOD'S KALEIDOSCOPE

Steve Smith

When my speck of green
turned the brown
of Job's dunghill
I looked up
to curse . . .
but then I saw
the reflection in God's eye.
Through his kaleidoscope
all turns are just as
beautiful.

NOAH

David Solway

He has a talent for uneasiness,
drinks too much coffee, chooses to rehearse
the nag and riddle of the universe;
he scans the clearest sky for cumulus
to cloud the heart, declares, in self-embrace,
the arch-perfectionist a candidate for grace.

How can he sit at table, and delight
in cream and figs, and smile? He glumly goes
against the bright ideal of repose,
the lesser peace of coasting in the light,
like Noah in his arcane discipline
troubling wife and neighbour with his prophetic din.

Though he may see what others do not see,
poetry's perception without power;
yet he abandons the sufficient hour
of milk and bread and apples from the tree
and dreams the hour the mind will not defraud
as he saws and he hammers, one eye on his god;

He dreams the distant and unplundered sea,
forgets the portrait on the mantelpiece,
the oaken trestle and the bolster-fleece
and all heroic domesticity;
he dreams the world of the kindred ships,
anticipates the pleasures of Apocalypse.

146

And is it all a figment of the blood—
this famished, unameliorable mind,
this sea-buffeted, salt-encrusted, blind
imagination calling down a flood?
He stacks his eclogues in unpublished heaps,
diviner of a world in which the dreamer reaps.

So let him itch and twitch, a weatherfrog,
and watch his fingers stain with nicotine.
The nervous poet contemplates a green
Sahara, and, when all is night and fog,
the greater peace of sensing in the dark
miraculous mountains for his uncompassed ark.

AFTER THE FLOOD

David Solway

After the flood, there was no rainbow in the sky.
The puzzled patriarch rubbed his eyes and looked again,
there was no rainbow anywhere to be seen.
There was no command, paternal and indulgent,
to be fruitful as the earth and multiply,
there was no sound anywhere to be heard
except the subversive grumbling of the animals.
He knew his master then to be whimsical and coy
and not averse to going to great lengths
to ruin a script or tweak the prompter's nose.
He wondered what to tell the waiting scribes.
After the flood, there was no rainbow in the sky.

148

MOSES

David Solway

By night a column of fire, and by day
a burning cloud precedes us, on the way
toward some promised land not of this earth
twenty centuries and more. Tired of birth
some have gone back, considering they can
return to the fleshpots of Canaan.
But our destination is not in time
nor the temple in place. Jerusalem,
heavenly city of transfigured stone,
the pearl of great price, shines beyond the sun.
Refined to a purer substance, annealed
in the kilns of doubt, a people steeled
and tested, vision clarified, can see
that Canaan is the new captivity.

JERICHO

David Solway

It is some time after Jericho.
I have been nourished
on sand and miracles.
I have fought my sum of battles.
My skin is tanned and cured,
a leather buckler.
And the Lord has spoken to me.
Now the rivers of this country
sing like cherubim
and the bees ooze honey.
My women bathe in milk
and bring me sweetmeats.
My garments are of purest wool.
And the Lord converses with me.
And yet I have no peace
though it is many years after Jericho.
Restless as a sentry who listens for rumours
I have begun to suspect that Jericho
is any occupied country.
I have begun to suspect that Jericho
will never fall.

THE CHOSEN PEOPLE

David Solway

They made amends like some embarrassed host:
the strange refineries all were smelted down,
reparations paid, and penitential
nightmares dreamed; judgments rendered in the town
the Press made famous would dispel the pall
that brooded on the mind. They claimed a most
unOvidian metamorphosis:
memory's stigmata healed by remorse;

yet cherished the disease in skull and bone,
with exemplary concentration
locked it up in ironclad resentments
and thought Jehovah luciferian,
while Capital and both the Testaments
blazed on, apocalyptic, in the brain.
Time must open every wound again
and ancient scars renew the ancient pain.

You put your trust in humour, money, prayers.
It seems you put your trust in anything
but the world's sweet incendiary hate.
Many, many tackle you, forcing
you to earth, but always you learn too late.
Construe the handwriting in newspapers.
Elucidate tattoos on burnished skin.
Mene, Mene, Tekel, Upharsin.

Renounce all profit for your prophets claim
an aching conscience is a monstrous thing;
and poets who explore each cave and cove
of unrequited hate, declare men sting
being loved beyond their means to love
and always take revenge on the sublime.
It needs all History to educate
a stubborn people: whom God loves men hate.

O they shall pay you back for Moses; owe
a debt of centuries for crippling Paul;
and for the great evangelist Saint Karl
whose gospel is become canonical
they shall return a universal snarl.
Once more you have been chosen. Columns glow
in the world's wilderness. Once more you learn
it is not gratitude but fire you earn.

For Bill Goodwin

WHY SHOULD I CARE ABOUT THE WORLD

Miriam Waddington

Gone is
the holiness
in where I
lived, my song.

Why should I care
what happens to
the world why
should I
broodingly
seek the cell of
holiness the
habit in where
I lived, my song?

(Your song
was only a few
ragged Scotsmen
in Kildonan, some
riff-raffy settlers,
half-breeds, Indians,
Galician labourers,
scraggly-ended
pee-smelling prairie
towns)

153

(it was a flat
stony mound
for a mountain
a silly tuft
of pine on
an island in
Lac du Bonnet,
berry-picking in a
buffalo summer
beside a wheat ocean
and jumping the
ditches brimming
with rain.)

Gone now; all
cracked open like
eggs at Easter
parted like three
feathers in a
bird's tail of wind.

And I can't even
go back to being
dirty Jew, to
hearing from the
conductor on the
Selkirk streetcar:
*your father is
a Bolshevik isn't
he little girl?*

154

This is a **very**
far very **long**
way to be away
from the holiness
in where I lived
my song.

155

FINDING AMOS IN JERUSALEM

Miriam Waddington

He gave me
golden stones
when I wanted
stories he gave
me silence
for my blindest
furies;

He withheld
his presence he
hid his face
I hunted the
city for his
hiding-place
and dug in the
rubble for his
smallest trace;

He was here he
was there he was
always nowhere
whether dragging
the wcight of
a beggar's feet
or folded away
in a stranger's
frown; yet everyone
swore they had
seen him pass not
an hour before.

Above the market
or under its roofs
I listened for
the sound of those
ancient hoofs
for ghostly wheels
in the narrow streets
splashing blood of
boys with the curse
of Greece while
Egypt's hate
burned a fiery path
to Damascus Gate.

He hid from me
in an olive grove
in a cold green pit
by the Nablus road
on a January day
in the winter sun;
he called from the
bunkers he shuddered
in caves and sent out
a whisper from layers
of stone: *God is Almighty
and God is One* while the
blue song of Islam told
of brothers betrayed
then fell broken-winged
from love's scaffold.

157

THIS YEAR IN JERUSALEM

Miriam Waddington

Other years Hannah
the woman who cleans
offices in Jerusalem
cursed the white sun
of Jerusalem because
it was not the green
sun of her village
in Poland.

This year that same
Hannah has something
to curse about; she
curses the Egyptians
and Assyrians who
killed the son she
brought to Jerusalem
from her village
in Poland.

158

And at dawn this year
the cats of Jerusalem
don't come anymore
to the steps of the
post-office to wait
for morning and the
charwomen to come
to work and feed them.

This year
even the cats know
there are too many
enemies.

159

WHEN WE MET

Miriam Waddington

When we met
the first time it was
really the last time,
we spoke to each other
in the lost tongues of
our parents' Europe;
whose piano did you play
that spring afternoon
in the shadowed house
near the mountain
and whose song was
I singing entirely
to myself?

Was I my mother?
Were you your father?
Did we meet on a street
in Odessa or a birch forest
on the Volga or was it at
the artificial lake I dug out
in miniature and planted round
with tall buttercups for trees
behind an old hotel
in Winnipeg?

Why did it take me
so long to find our
lost languages,
to learn our songs?

THE TRANSPLANTED: SECOND GENERATION

Miriam Waddington

Some day my son
you'll go to Leningrad,
you'll see grey canals
under arches and bridges,
you'll see green-and-white
walls of winter palaces,
you'll visit the towered
prison across the river
and smell the breath
of dead revolutions;
perhaps you'll even hear
the ghostly marching of
sailors in empty avenues
and catch the ebbing sound
of their wintry slogans.

You'll remember
that Jews could spend no
nights in Leningrad when
it was called St. Petersburg;
Jews moved with documents
shuffled and crushed like
paper; the Yiddish writer
Peretz was met by his friend
Anski at Leningrad station;
he delivered his lecture
to a crowded hall then spent
the night in a suburb
twenty miles away.

Some day my son
when you are in Leningrad
you'll see those palaces
and turning fountains,
you'll stare at pendulums
of gilded saintliness,
count kingly treasure-hoards
in glass museum-cases;
then you'll remember
Nova Scotia's pasture-lands
its clumps of blueberries
and our August mornings
on hidden lakes at the end
of logging roads.

And some day my son
just there in Leningrad
across those distances
you will feel my Winnipeg:
its lakes of fish its skies
of snow and its winds of
homelessness will stir
something in your blood;
then will you hear forgotten
languages and you will read
the troubled map of our
long ancestral geography
in your own son's eyes.

BY THE SEA: FOR A.M. KLEIN

Miriam Waddington

His grief it fell and fell;
he mourned that his brain
could never be like new—
a seamless whole again.

He polished it with spit
and sealed the cracks with glue,
he pinned it to the air—
yet away it flew.

He caught it in a net
of silken words and wit,
but his broken brain
was fragmented and split.

He quilted it with grass
and anchored it with ships,
he sailed tilting words,
they foundered on his lips.

He dropped a silver line
into the tides of verse,
and found his broken brain
had hooked it to a curse.

So he called the angels down
from balconies of sky,
they emptied out his life,
they would not let him die.

Then someone drained the ponds
in his unlettered land,
and strangers hid the road
beneath a mile of sand,

Apollo's golden ear
was sealed against his cries,
his lonely broken brain
was barred from paradise.

His grief it falls and falls
on green fields and on white,
he rocks his broken brain
that never mended right,

And sings his silent song
to earth and tree and stone;
we hear it when we hear
the rain beat on the stone.

The rain beats on the stone:
but how many recognize
his broken brain, his fear,
are nothing but our own?

164

THE DEATH OF THE PARTISAN GIRL: RUSSIA

Tom Wayman

There must have been a time when everything to you
was clear as iron: that the kitchen of bread must pass
to the gun-cleaning rag, attics and the low sheds around
    farms.
Your child became a motorcycle
a stretch of road, a wire and birch trees.

And when they had you, time became German.
If someone could only have whispered
you will be held four days, raped twice
beaten for this many minutes. But no-one said that.
So you could not know they would not
smash you in the face for another hour
press their bloody sperm into you in turn
all afternoon, and burn your nipples and tongue with
    cigarettes
every day at six o'clock for a week.

Then they killed you. Someone took a photograph
of your body. Your eyelids were swollen shut.
They put the picture in a book, and years later
in another country, a man you could not possibly know
looks at your beautiful face and becomes confused.

He believes that when you knew words were useless
you opened a knapsack and took out a terrible metal canister.
His fingers are shaking now, holding only paper.
Who can touch you? You were in agony, that your brother
    could say
my older sister was killed in 1943, the Nazis
tortured her, your niece could say *my aunt*
whom I never knew, died in the war, your parents
could say *there was another daughter, but she's gone*

And when it happened, your cause was lost.
Now your butchers readjust themselves on a sofa somewhere
to be interviewed by sympathetic pencils.
You, partisan, no-one can forgive. You are dead.
All we can do is put a black-and-white photo of the husk of
    dead meat
that was you, hung from a rope, in a book and forget it.

But I intend to remember.

166

WHERE I COME FROM: GRANDFATHER

Tom Wayman

A dead man. A dead person,
who ran away from the London Jews and joined
the Royal Sussex Regiment, shipping east
in an old three-decker to India, his pay-book
stamped *Church of England*, under his new
English name. The Regiment
taught him grammar and arithmetic
while he garrisoned the North West Frontier,
had the collar of his uniform shot off
and was promoted to corporal, but one night
an officer returned to camp drunk
without the proper challenge, so every NCO on duty
—including him—got reduced to the ranks.

Back in England, they say he and his brother
stood in Trafalgar Square and tossed
to decide who would go to Canada and who to South Africa.
Thus my grandfather was awarded Toronto
and a job as a machine-operator
for Tip Top Tailors, a wife, a family,
a death, and another wife,
a house on Borden Street eleven and a half feet wide
in a street of Jews, with Jews living upstairs.

He also got a strike in the midst of the Depression
and only went back to his machine during
another war. In 1945 he was chosen
Inner Guard of the Mozirir Sick and Burial Society
—a social and self-help club for ex-Russian Jews
which he was too, if you went back far enough
though locally he was known for his speech and military
    bearing
as "the Mayor of Borden Street" or "the Englishman."

In his last years, he refused to give up the house
though he was sick a number of times, and though
the street began to fill with south Italians.
A kid from the neighbourhood prepared a meal for him
    most days
in return for a little money. And his room
began to hold all the clutter and dust of the single elderly
    poor:
faded snapshots and photographs, a calendar, the same few
    dishes
used every day, a television continually muttering
and mumbling to itself, the bed rumpled and half-made.

When he died, few on the street knew him.
He had to be carried into death by
a step-cousin's band of musicians
who had attended the funeral out of courtesy
and stayed to bear the old man to the grave.

168

They lifted him into a small shed at the edge of the cemetery
and came out and stood around, while shards of porcelain
    were put
on his ears, eyes, nose and mouth
to show that in the grave nothing is heard,
nothing seen, nothing smelled, nothing tasted
and nothing said. The first handful of sand from the grave
was put into the coffin, to show
earth to the earth.

            And standing at the open gravesite
the young rabbi with the red band in his hat
who never knew any of us in life or death
but managed anyway to make up a little message about my
    grandfather
which actually could have been about anybody
now led my father in the halting, word-for-word
repetition of the Kaddish.
Then they turned on the machine for lowering the coffin
and flung a mat of synthetic grass
over the slowly descending box, as inside
what was left of what had been my grandfather went down
wrapped in the step-cousin's shawl.

Seven days the candle burned for him: seven days
seven years ago now. And from my grandfather
I got my father, my name,
the ring they took off his body that he had been given
when he made Inner Guard, and I got
a cheap disposable yarmulka handed out from a tray
at the funeral, a skullcap I still have
scrunched up in one pocket of a coat in a closet
kept in case I ever need it again.

169

WAYMAN IN LOVE

Tom Wayman

At last Wayman gets the girl into bed.
He is locked in one of those embraces
so passionate his left arm is asleep
when suddenly he is bumped in the back.
"Excuse me," a voice mutters, thick with German.
Wayman and the girl sit up astounded
as a furry gentleman in boots and a frock coat
climbs in under the covers.

"My name is Doktor Marx," the intruder announces
settling his neck comfortably on the pillow.
"I'm here to consider for you the cost of a kiss."
He pulls out a notepad. "Let's see now,
we have the price of the mattress, this room must be rented,
your time off work, groceries for two,
medical fees in case of accidents . . . ."

"Look," Wayman says,
"couldn't we do this later?"
The philosopher sighs, and continues: "You are affected too,
    Miss.
If you are not working, you are going to resent
your dependent position. This will influence,
I assure you, your most intimate moments . . . ."

"Doctor, please," Wayman says. "All we want
is to be left alone."
But another beard, more nattily dressed,
is also getting into the bed.
There is a shifting and heaving of bodies
as everyone wriggles out room for themselves.
"I want you to meet a friend from Vienna,"
Marx says. "This is Doktor Freud."

The newcomer straightens his glasses,
peers at Wayman and the girl.
"I can see," he begins,
"that you two have problems . . . ."

THE SURVIVORS

David Weisstub

My tender child
your secrets are mine,
I knew you not,
yet do I tell you
that we are together,
that you are not alone.
I know that Nazi hand
that smote your mother's smile
and dragged her inners for artifacts,
I saw the bayonet
that stole your brother's brain
and tossed it to the wind
laughing and burying a shot
to leave no trace.
Child, while your eyes shine dimly
in the dream of hands stretching
row on row
your people send prayers, emissaries
from the dead
that go on living.
Child o dear child
be comforted.

WIDOWHOOD

Shulamis Yelin

Immigrant under cloudless skies,
I'm free to come and go—
can shop and pay for,
travel,
indulge myself in haute cuisine,
enjoy the galleries,
concerts,
observe the sports as natives do.

But I have never learned the language of the land,
attend but films sub-titled in my native tongue,
and plays for me are baffling pantomimes!

My days are plagued
with constant translation
from sense to sense,
from one tongue to another,
missing joke, nuance,
idiom and inflection—
coldly hungering for home.

173

ZEROING IN

Shulamis Yelin

Death can come softly:
knock at the door, enter without bidding,
and certain but polite,
relieve you of your duties.

Or lateness can happen:
the heart may tire of patient waiting,
and slowly, metronomically,
stop.

Or wish can conquer:
a patch of green recurring every springtime
on earth, too early
bedding down one's seed.

But to me: let it come
side-saddle, ambling.
On my way from finished business
let me meet Death
and sign a signal contract:
quid pro quo—for fullness—
merchandise received
and payment duly met.

Avi Boxer was born and raised in Montreal. His poems began to appear in little magazines in the nineteen-fifties. To date he has published one collection, *No Address*, 1971.

Born and raised in Los Angeles, Mick Burrs moved to Canada in 1965 and now lives in Regina. He is the editor of *Going to War: Found Poems of the Metis People*, 1975, and the author of three collections of poetry, including *Moving In From Paradise*, 1976, and *The Blue Pools of Paradise*, 1983.

Leonard Cohen was born and raised in Montreal. His first book, *Let Us Compare Mythologies*, 1956, initiated the McGill Poetry Series. Cohen's subsequent collections include *The Spice-Box of Earth*, 1961, *Flowers for Hitler*, 1964 and *Selected Poems, 1956-68*, 1968. He has written two novels as well as *Death of a Lady's Man*, a work of prose and poetry, which appeared in 1978. *Book of Mercy*, 1984, is his latest collection. His many recorded songs and compositions enjoy a wide international following and his writings have been translated into a number of languages.

Stanley Cooperman was born in Brooklyn, New York and was educated in the United States. He came to Canada in the sixties and published a number of collections, including *Cappelbaum's Dance*, 1970, and *Cannibals*, 1972. *Canadian Gothic and Other Poems* appeared posthumously in 1976.

Born and raised in Dublin, Hyman Edelstein came to Canada in 1912. For most of his life he worked as an editor and writer and lived in Ottawa and Montreal. He was the author of eleven books of poetry, among them *Canadian Lyrics and Other Poems*, 1916, *Selected Poems*, 1931, and *Spirit of Israel and Other Poems*, 1950.

Born and raised in Montreal, George Ellenbogen now teaches at Bentley College in Massachusetts. His first collection was published in the McGill Poetry Series in 1957. *The Night Unstones* appeared in 1971.

Susan Glickman was born and raised in Montreal. She has worked as a book editor and now teaches at the University of Toronto. Her first collection, *Complicity*, was published in 1983.

Born in Brockville, Ontario, Artie Gold was raised in Montreal, where he continues to live. His most recent collection is *before Romantic Words*, 1979.

Phyllis Gotlieb was born and educated in Toronto. She is the author of four novels, including *Why Should I Have All the Grief?*, 1969, and four collections of poetry. *The Works: Collected Poems* appeared in 1978.

K.V. Hertz was born and raised in Montreal. His poetry and short fiction have both appeared in many Canadian and American magazines. *Eurithrea*, a satirical prose work, was published in 1973.

Born in Budapest, Hungary, George Jonas arrived in Canada in 1956. His collections include *The Happy Hungry Man*, 1970, and *Cities*, 1973. With Barbara Amiel he wrote the story of Christine Demeter in 1977 and he has since written a novel, several plays and a documentary. He works as a radio producer for the CBC in Toronto.

Gertrude Katz grew up in Montreal. She compiled an anthology of work by prison inmates entitled *The Time Gatherers*, 1970. Her most recent collection of poems, *Duet*, appeared in 1982.

A.M. Klein was born in Ratno in the Ukraine and was brought to Canada in 1910, when he was only a year old. He was educated in Montreal and lived there until his death. He practised law for a number of years and edited *The Canadian Jewish Chronicle* from 1938 to 1955, as well as teaching at McGill from 1945 to 1948. *The Rocking Chair and Other Poems* won the Governor General's Award in 1948. His *Collected Poems*, edited by Miriam Waddington, appeared posthumously in 1974. The first volume of his collected works was published in 1982, the second a year later.

Born in Roumania, Irving Layton was brought to Canada at an early age and was raised in Montreal. For many years he taught there before he moved to Toronto to teach at York University, where he remained until his retirement. He has published more than 40 books of poetry, the most recent of which is *The Gucci Bag*, 1983. His first volume of collected poems, *A Red Carpet for the Sun*, won the Governor General's Award in 1959. His selected poems have appeared in Spanish and Italian translations.

Born and raised in Ottawa, Norman Levine was educated at McGill University. He lived in England for many years but now makes his home in Toronto. He has published three collections of poetry, as well as several volumes of short fiction. His *Selected Stories* appeared in 1975.

Eli Mandel was born in Estevan, Saskatchewan and was educated at the Universities of Saskatchewan and Toronto. He has taught at the University of Alberta and now teaches at York University. He has edited a number of anthologies and written several critical studies, including one on Irving Layton. His *An Idiot Joy* won the Governor General's Award for 1967. His most recent collection is *Life Sentence*, 1981. His *Selected Poems* appeared in the same year.

Born and raised in Montreal, Seymour Mayne has taught at the Hebrew University of Jerusalem, and now teaches at the University of Ottawa. He has edited a number of critical texts in Canadian literature and translated poetry from the Yiddish. A volume of new and selected poems, *The Impossible Promised Land*, appeared in 1981, and *Vanguard of Dreams*, his selected poems in Hebrew translation, in 1984.

Born and raised in the United States, Malcolm Miller graduated from McGill University and taught in Montreal for a number of years. He has published three collections of poetry, the most recent, *The Summer of the True Gods*, in 1978.

Born in Montreal, Henry Moscovitch attended McGill and Columbia Universities. His first book of poems, *The Serpent Ink*, 1956, was published by Contact Press. *New Poems*, 1982, is his most recent collection.

Sharon H. Nelson grew up in Montreal and was educated at Sir George Williams University. Her most recent collection is *Mad Women & Crazy Ladies*, 1983. She has taught at Concordia University in Montreal.

A native Montrealer, Nathan Ralph was first published in the little magazines, *First Statement* and *Contemporary Verse*. His chapbook, *Twelve Poems*, appeared in 1941, and a book of poems, *Coffee and Bitters*, in 1947.

Janis Rapoport was raised and educated in Toronto. She has written several plays and is currently editor of the literary magazine, *Ethos*. Her most recent book of poems is *Winter Flowers*, 1979.

Born in Toronto, Joe Rosenblatt now lives on Vancouver Island. *Top Soil*, a collection of his best work to date, won the Governor General's Award for 1976. Since 1970 he has edited the quarterly *Jewish Dialog*. His most recent book, *Brides of the Stream*, appeared in 1983.

Helene Rosenthal was born in Toronto, but now lives and teaches in British Columbia. Her first book, *Peace is an Unknown Continent*, was published in 1967. New and selected poems were published in 1975 under the title, *Listen to the Old Mother*.

Born and educated in Toronto, Nancy-Gay Rotstein has published two collections of poems, *Through the Eyes of a Woman*, 1975, and *Taking Off*, 1979.

Ray Shankman was born in Toronto and now teaches at Vanier College in Montreal. His poems have appeared in a number of literary magazines and anthologies.

Joseph Sherman grew up in Nova Scotia. He was educated at the University of New Brunswick and has taught at Collège Saint-Louis-Maillet in Edmundston. His two most recent collections are *Chaim the Slaughterer*, 1974, and *Lords of Shouting*, 1982. He lives in Charlottetown and edits *Arts Atlantic*.

Born in Toronto, Kenneth Sherman teaches at Sheridan College in Brampton, Ontario. He has published three collections, of which the most recent is *Words for Elephant Man*, 1983.

Steve Smith grew up in Montreal. His collection, *God's Kaleidoscope*, was published in the McGill Poetry Series just before his untimely death.

David Solway was born in Montreal and now teaches at John Abbott College in Ste.-Anne de Bellevue, Quebec. He edited the anthology *4 Montreal Poets* in 1973, and his most recent collections include *Mephistopheles and the Astronaut,* 1979, a book of verse for children and *Stones in Water,* 1983. His *Selected Poems* appeared in 1982.

Miriam Waddington was born in Winnipeg and educated at the Universities of Toronto and Pennsylvania. For two decades she taught at York University. She is the author of eleven collections of poetry, the most recent of which is *The Visitants,* 1981. She has written a study of A.M. Klein and edited his collected poems, and translated poetry and prose from the Yiddish. A collection of stories, *Summer at Lonely Beach,* was published in 1982.

Born in Hawkesbury, Ontario, Tom Wayman grew up in BC, where he attended the University of British Columbia. He has published several books of poems, including *Waiting for Wayman,* 1973, and *Counting the Hours,* 1983. He has taught at David Thompson University Centre in Nelson, BC and currently teaches for the Kootenay School of Writing in Vancouver.

Born in Port Arthur, Ontario, David Weisstub was raised in Winnipeg and now teaches law at York University in Toronto. He has published one collection, *Heaven Take My Hand,* in 1968.

Born, raised and educated in Montreal, Shulamis Yelin has taught there for many years. She has published one collection, *Seeded in Sinai,* 1975, and a book of short autobiographical sketches, *Shulamis: Stories from a Montreal Childhood,* 1983.

ACKNOWLEDGEMENTS

Avi Boxer: reprinted by permission of the author.

Mick Burrs: reprinted by permission of the author.

Leonard Cohen: reprinted by permission of McClelland and Stewart, Ltd.

Stanley Cooperman: reprinted by permission of Oberon Press.

Hyman Edelstein: reprinted by permission of Nat Edelstein.

George Ellenbogen: reprinted by permission of the author.

Susan Glickman: reprinted by permission of the author.

Artie Gold: reprinted by permission of the author.

Phyllis Gotlieb: reprinted by permission of the author.

K.V. Hertz: reprinted by permission of the author.

George Jonas: reprinted by permission of the author.

Gertrude Katz: reprinted by permission of the author.

A.M. Klein: reprinted by permission of Colman and Sandor Klein.

Irving Layton: reprinted by permission of McClelland and Stewart, Ltd.

Norman Levine: reprinted by permission of the author.

Eli Mandel: reprinted by permission of the author.

Seymour Mayne: reprinted by permission of the author.

Malcolm Miller: reprinted by permission of the author.

Henry Moscovitch: reprinted by permission of the author.

Sharon H. Nelson: reprinted by permission of the author.

Nathan Ralph: reprinted by permission of Dvora Marcuse.

Janis Rapoport: reprinted by permission of the author.

Joe Rosenblatt: reprinted by permission of the author.

Helene Rosenthal: reprinted by permission of the author.

Nancy-Gay Rotstein: reprinted by permission of the author.

Ray Shankman: reprinted by permission of the author.